New England's S

This book is dedicated to my bro
Master of Salem, Massachusetts.

The Derelict — oil by Marsall Johnson,
photo courtesy The Peabody Museum, Salem, MA

ISBN 0-916787-04-4

Cover Photo:

Painting of famous navigator Nathaniel Bowditch by Harold Schmidt, courtesy of the John Hancock Mutual Life Insurance Company, Boston, MA.

Printed in Canada

INTRODUCTION

When ships were the only connecting link between continents and often the only source of communication between countries, sailoring was among the most honored of professions. The captain of the ship was "master" not only of his vessel and crew, but in the community as well. He brought needed supplies, new fascinating items from abroad, and often, news of great interest and importance from people living far over the sea. He was usually the wealthiest of men, respected by all in his home port. The old sea masters' mansions of Salem, Massachusetts give witness to the wealth and power of these men. Captain Elias Derby of Salem was America's first millionaire.

Yet, there wasn't a captain or seaman who ever left port who didn't ponder the possibility of never returning. The vast oceans are treacherous, able to pound a ship to pieces, leaving her a derelict to drift helplessly, her crew dying of thirst and hunger. Seamen could fall overboard in a storm; drop from the rigging; be attacked by pirates, savages or an enemy in some strange foreign port. There were many mishaps and tragedies that could befall them, but the most terrifying of all was to have their ship sink from under their feet. Just the thought of breakers exploding over a reef and a ship lifting to the crackle of splintering wood filled them with fear. When steel replaced wood and ships cruised under as well as over the waves, the dangers did not diminish, nor did the hidden fears disappear. Fear has oftentimes been the source of bravery and heroics at sea, but it has also produced panic and cowardice on the high seas, especially when that fear becomes a reality.

These stories are about New England seamen— the brave and the cowardly, the indolent and industrious — and the ships in which they sailed. They are true sagas about the improbable, unusual and sometimes seemingly impossible. **New England's STRANGE SEA SAGAS**, the fifth book in Chandler-Smith's Collectible Classic Series, is really about the sea — her mischievous moods and her malevolent mysteries — mysteries that have perplexed New Englanders since the Virginia bound **MAYFLOWER** was blown off her course in a storm and mistakenly landed at Plymouth.

Bob Cahill

I
THE DORYMAN

To the old New England fishermen there never was, nor will there ever be, a more seaworthy open boat than the double-ended dory — often referred to as, *"the rowboat with two bows."* There aren't many fishing dories along the New England coast today, but in the 1800s and early 1900s they were most prevalent, especially in Gloucester, Massachusetts and at America's favorite fishing grounds, the Grand Banks.

At the Banks, a small fleet of dories, each measuring 12 to 20 feet in length, carrying two fishermen apiece, would be accompanied by a large sailing vessel — usually a schooner — called the *"mother ship."* The schooner would drop off each dory in the morning within hailing distance of each other, and pick them up before nightfall — following the same procedure day after day until the hold of the mother ship was filled with fish. Then, with dories in tow or hauled aboard, the schooner would head the hundreds of miles back to shore with the combined catch — halibut and cod were the main catch of the dory fishermen.

Many times while fishing at the Banks, the dories would drift away from each other in storms or from the forceful pull of a 100 pound halibut. The mother ship and sometimes the dories were supplied with a horn to be sounded by the fishermen if they drifted out of sight of each other or were lost in a fog. God help the dorymen who were not picked up by the schooner at the end of the day, for their alternatives were to drift in the open sea in hopes of being spotted by a passing ship or of being picked up by another fishing vessel, or to attempt the seemingly impossible — to row the 100 or more miles back to the mainland in their little open boat.

Such was the fate of two men from Gloucester as they fished Burgeo Bank one wild wet January in 1883. The mother ship, **FEARS**, had dropped off Howard Blackburn and his dory-mate Thomas *"Willie"* Welch as morning snow flurries spat across the wide expanse of rolling grey water. By late afternoon the sky darkened, and the snow fell thicker — Blackburn's 19-footer drifted away from the other boats. Willie, who was only 19 years old, picked up the horn and blew it into the snowflakes, and he kept blowing until he was blue in the face. They listened for the sound of a horn from the mother ship or from another dory but heard only the whistling wind and the hiss of snow on the water. At nightfall the wind picked up, splashing frigid water over the bow. Shivering from cold and fear, young Willie and 23 year old Howard Blackburn decided on their course of action. A Nor'east squall was upon them, and they were being pushed further out to sea — the storm would continue for hours, maybe days, and there was little chance of another vessel spotting them. They had only one chance to survive, and that was to take the longshot — row the 100 or more miles against the wind to Newfoundland, the nearest landfall.

The dorymen were dressed in thick, water-resistant slickers called oilskins, sweaters, wool pants, wool mittens and boots. With the constant exercise of rowing they might, thought Blackburn, keep their bodies from freezing. The dory was equipped with a compass, a bailing pan, a club for killing fish, trawl lines, oars and fishbait. Keeping the heavy halibut aboard would only slow their progress, they concluded, so the entire day's catch, save one codfish, was thrown overboard. When they got hungry they could eat the fishbait and the cod. Howard and Willie took turns — one rowing while the other bailed. Day and night they rowed without stopping for fear they would drift. Neither man dared sleep for fear he would freeze to death. After the third day, Willie gave up. *"We can't live 'til morning,"* he said, *"I must sleep,"* and he closed his eyes forever.

Blackburn took the oars, determined that he would not put them down until he reached shore. He could hardly feel his hands, and his arms and legs ached with almost unbearable pain. He longed for a drink of water, but even the ice caked to the bow tasted salty. *"Stroke, feather, stroke, feather, stroke,"* he mumbled rhythmically to the frozen corpse of Willie Welch. He could lessen the weight by dumping Willie overboard, but he couldn't bring himself to do it. Salt spray began to ice up along the gunwhales, and his wet mittens were caked with ice too. Pausing to remove some of the ice, he lost one of his mittens overboard. He rowed on, wearing the remaining mitten on one hand for an hour, then transferring it to the other. During one of the transfers, he lost his second mitten overboard. His numb fingers kept slipping from the oars; now his greatest fear was that he might lose an oar. He could not control his hands — there was no feeling left in them. All was lost unless he made a desperate gruesome decision; he must give up his hands for the oars.

Quickly, before he could let himself change his mind, he dipped both hands into the sea, then shaping them as best he could to fit the oar handles, he held them to the wind. Within minutes his hands were frozen solid. He fit them to the oars and rowed on through the storm-tossed waters of the North Atlantic. Then the flesh began flaking off his fingers like fishscales. Within hours the skin was gone from his hands, yet he pushed the dory on inch by inch towards land. His fear now was that the pressure of pulling on the oars might snap his fingers off.

After five days and nights of constant rowing, Howard Blackburn spotted the misty low-lying coast of Newfoundland. Tears froze on his weary face. *"We made it,"* he shouted to Willie. He rowed on into a desolate cove at the head of a river and beached the dory. Then came the tedious process of dipping his hands into the sea to melt the ice that molded his fingers to the oars — he expected pain, but felt nothing. Hardly able to stand, he half crawled up the beach until he spied an old fishing shack. He kicked in the door of the shack with his frostbitten feet. Inside the shack was a stove and firewood— then he found the most precious item of all, flint and tinder to start a fire. Howard's skeletal fingers could not bring a spark to the flint. He even tried using his toes, but they were frozen numb too. Without fire, he thought, he could not sleep, for it would mean certain death from the cold, even though now he was under the protective roof of the shack. He had an overpowering urge to sleep, and after his grueling ordeal at sea, Howard Blackburn gave up the fight — he laid down on the floor of the shack to sleep and surely die.

To his surprise he woke up in the shack many hours later, shivering uncontrollably. He walked outside and ate snow until his mouth and tongue burned from it, and he doubled over with stomach cramps. He crawled back to the dory and set off again in hopes of finding help. After rowing some six miles he spotted three fishermen walking along the ice at the river's edge. He shouted to them and rowed in. He had brought Willie back home to the place of his birth, Borgeo, Newfoundland. The men were from a nearby poverty stricken fishing village only a few miles from Borgeo. They carried Howard to one of their fishing shacks where he remained for almost four months being nursed back to health by the wives of the fishermen. He was fed fish and dog meat, all that the poor folks had to offer, and his wounds were healed with the powder of ground-up muscle shells. During his recovery period, however, every finger of both hands, except for a thumb, fell off, as did six of his toes and the heel of one foot. He returned home to Gloucester on June 15, 1883 to a hero's welcome.

Howard's friends helped him open a tobacco shop and pub in Gloucester; but to the widows and orphans of Gloucester fishermen who had died at sea, he donated the hundreds of dollars he received from various benefits in his honor. When Blackburn's Tavern prospered, he sent food and clothing every Christmas to the poor fishermen and their families at Borgeo. Although crippled for life, Howard Blackburn's life of adventure on the high seas was far from over. He headed an expedition voyage to the Klondike gold rush in 1897 and made a solo voyage across the Atlantic to Gloucester, England in 1899. His *"fingerless-toeless"* lone crossing from Gloucester to Gloucester earned him a British welcome equal to the one he received from his home town 16 years earlier when he returned from Borgeo. Howard Blackburn died on November 4, 1932 — in his sleep.

"But t'weren't just the blood and guts determination nor just the providence of the All-Mighty that saved Blackburn in that open boat," old Gloucester fishermen will tell you, *"t'was the dory, by God, t'was the dory."*

The Dorymen, oil by Harvey Dudin, courtesy John Hancock Mutual Life Insurance Company, Boston. (Insert) Howard Blackburn, photo courtesy The Cape Ann Historical Association, Gloucester, MA.

II
CRAZY CARGOES

"Old Bet" was the name of the hideous beast that stepped ashore from the schooner **AMERICA** in the autumn of 1795. Women screamed and fainted, children ran home to hide from it. It was the biggest animal anyone in the United States had ever seen. It had *"enormous leafy ears, tough leathery skin and a long nose that scraped the ground,"* reported the *Salem Gazette.* It was an elephant, the first to America. The strange beast created quite a stir on the docks when it made its debut, arriving first in New York and then at Salem, Massachusetts. It had been stuffed aboard the **AMERICA** by her captain, Jacob Crowninshield, as a joke to surprise his four brothers. First mate Nat Hathorne, father of famous novelist Nathaniel Hawthorne, grudgingly became its caretaker during the long voyage. *"Took aboard punkins and greens for the elephant on board"* Hathorne wrote in the ship's log on October 25, 1795, but once Old Bet was put on display in the Salem marketplace, at 25 cents a peek for adults and 12½ cents for children, it was fed greens along with rum and porter wine; it soon became a 3,000 pound drunk. Captain Crowninshield didn't mind though, for he had sold the elephant when he arrived in America for $10,000.

Another unusual creature, the first in America, arrived at Salem on the brig **THREE SISTERS** in May of 1787. *"It is a young bird with an exceedingly long neck,"* reported the *Salem Mercury, "about the size of a turkey."* It was an ostrich, and actually two had been shipped from Africa by Captain Sanders in hopes of breeding them in New England, but the male bird died in transit.

There were many marvels and curiosities that came into New England ports in the years following the Revolutionary War, for it was then that war privateers were converted into merchant vessels, and courageous privateersmen became merchant mariners — braving wild wind and wave to explore uncharted seas and to visit far-away places with strange sounding names. It was a time when, if anything moved in or out of this young nation of ours, it moved over water — and there was plenty that America wanted to buy and sell. New Englanders venturing throughout the world peddling their wares were called *"Yankee traders"*; many foreigners thought places like Newburyport, Boston and Salem were separate nations. *"Certainly, with so many ships coming here from Salem,"* commented one Sumatran rajah to a sea captain, *"I cannot believe it is only one small village in America."* Between 1795 and 1812 from Salem alone, 179 vessels visited Sumatra continuously, taking on cargoes of pepper. Within seven years following the Revolution, New England's Yankee traders opened American trade with Russia, China, India, Africa, Arabia and South America. Round and round the world they traveled; carrying cargoes of everything and anything; snooping into one foreign port here and exploring another hidden harbor there; buying, selling and trading; but most importantly, finding out what items the foreigners needed or desired in order that they might bring it on the next trip.

The Yankee mariners soon learned that *"Ginseng,"* a weed growing wild in the woods, was considered a curative herb by the Chinese, who craved it. They especially desired the ginseng root, often shaped in the form of a miniature human being, which, when eaten or added in powder form to tea, enhanced their sexual desires and abilities, they thought. American doctors declared that ginseng was useless as a medicine and as an aphrodisiac, but that didn't dissuade New England farmers or sailors (when they were home) from scouring the woods for the leafy plants, digging them up, roots and all, to be packed aboard ships heading for the Orient. Although ginseng grows in Asia, it is prevalent in America from the Canadian border to New Orleans. It once brought hundreds of thousands of dollars in profits to the Yankee traders; however, New Englanders stopped rummaging through the forests for it about 100 years ago. Ironically, Midwesterners picked up the ginseng gathering avocation about the time New Englanders were giving it up. They continue to harvest it; and no wonder, for ginseng now sells for $130 per pound. The fragile forest lands of Iowa were becoming so mutilated by ginseng hunters, that a law was recently passed in that state banning the digging of ginseng except for three weeks in autumn. The Chinese still crave it, and America still exports it, shipping 132 metric tons of it to Hong Kong in 1983 — a cargo worth $47,500,000.

Another Oriental delicacy, revealed to the Yankee traders just prior to the turn of the 19th century, was a worm — a slimy, repulsive eight inch long sea worm called *"beche-de-mer."* The Chinese couldn't get enough of it. They ate the worms boiled or dried and often added as flavoring in soups. The worms — sea slugs — live in tidal pools and on coral reefs in the tropics, and although the Yankee mariners knew they could make fabulous profits gathering them and shipping them in bulk to China, beche-de-mer wasn't that easy to find in quantity. New England sailors searched every tropical island reef and atoll from the West Indies to Africa for the little brown slugs, realizing they were worth their weight in gold. They weren't found in abundance, however, until the brig **ACTIVE** returned to Salem on March 27, 1812, when her captain reported that the Fiji Islands were teeming with beche-de-mer. Word spread through the town like wild-fire — that was the good news. The bad news was that the Fiji Islanders were headhunters, and the food they craved was human flesh — especially white meat.

It wasn't the fear of being roasted at the stake or boiled in a pot that delayed the New Englanders from sailing to the Fijis; but they were at war with the British again, and merchant vessels were temporarily converted back into privateers. After the war, Salem merchant mariners cautiously approached Tanoa, King of the Fiji Islands, for permission to harvest the precious worms, which the islanders called "*trepang.*" For a few tools, some shiny trinkets and a couple of jugs of rum, the Salem sailors were allowed not only to gather the worms along the shore, but to set up pot-houses on the beaches where trepang could be boiled or smoked before delivery to the Chinese. The first ship to sail away from Kandora in the Fiji Islands, her hold filled with these cured, edible worms, was the **CLAY** of Salem. One of her sailors, Jim Magoun, was left behind at Kandora to live with the cannibals. He remained there for years as an agent for the Yankee traders. If the British tried to muzzle in on the American worm business, Jim Magoun was there to inform the Fiji king how tasty an Englishman could be when properly boiled in his own juices.

Jim Magoun won the love of the Fiji king and the respect of the other natives. One day he dove into the water and saved the king, who, drunk on rum, fell out of his dugout canoe and was going under for the third time. He also cured many natives during an island epidemic. Using his "*white man's medicine*" and laudanum, he pulled an aching tooth from the man-eating jaws of the king's son, Thakombau, relieving his pain. Jim became the white witch doctor of the Fiji Islands; but it was the Yankee traders, to protect their own interests, who paid handsomely for his services. However, there was one native in the Fijis who didn't like Magoun, and that was Barbadee, the tribe's wizened old witch doctor. To him, Magoun was an occupational threat.

William Driver, also from Salem and first-mate aboard the **CLAY** when she collected the valuable cargo of beche-de-mer at Kandora, returned in command of his own ship in 1883. Magoun had mentioned to Driver during his first visit that Salem sea captains and merchants were realizing a $30,000 annual profit on the slimy worms, and Driver decided he wanted a piece of the profits. Driver anchored his vessel, the brig **CHARLES DOGGET**, offshore while he and his crew with some hired natives collected the worms and cured them in the beach pot-houses. However, two members of the crew, while wandering in the Fiji village, came upon old Barbadee the witch doctor in the midst of one of his frenzied heathen ceremonies. The crewmen laughed at his antics, which infuriated Barbadee and sent him racing through the village, jabbering hysterically to his tribesmen. Jim Magoun arrived to call away the teasing sailors, but he was too late. Barbadee had the natives stirred up, telling them that the sailors had insulted the gods and should therefore be killed and eaten as a sacrifice. When the Fiji king agreed, Magoun realized that Driver and his crew were in big trouble.

Driver with his first mate, Dan Ames, and the rest of the crew were at the pot-house when they heard Barbadee screeching and saw Jim Magoun racing down the beach, frantically shouting to them to get to their boats. The Fiji headhunters were following close behind, wielding long spears and knives, Barbadee cheering them on. A native caught up with Magoun and speared him in the side. Ames took out a pistol he kept strapped to his waist and shot the native. Magoun stuck the same spear that had stabbed him into the belly of a second blood-thirsty native who tried to kill him. As the crew retreated to the longboats, some of them were involved in hand-to-hand combat with the Fijis, while others were struck down by spears or slashed with knives. Bill Driver and Ames went to Jim Majoun's aid as the headhunters swarmed down from the village. As they dragged Magoun to one of the boats, Ames was struck with a spear in the right thigh, and Driver's right arm was sliced by a longknife, but he managed to wrestle the knife from the native and stick him in the stomach. They managed to push off the boats, and with darts, arrows and spears splashing around them, they made it to their anchored ship. Five of their crewmen, including second mate Shipman and the two men who had provoked Barbadee, were captured or killed by the Fiji headhunters. Bill Driver wasted little time in putting on full sail and heading his brig to the Phillipines. Jim Magoun, after spending years with the Fiji Islanders, was on his way back to New England. When he reached Salem, his pert comment to the disappointed merchants was apt, *"If I had stayed behind, I'd have gone to pot."* Thus, New England's thriving worm business came to an end.

About the same time Magoun, Ames and Driver were fending off cannibals determined to have them for dinner, the Boston ship **TUSCANY** was sailing up the Hoogly River in Calcutta, India with a strange, secretive 180-ton cargo procured only a few miles from the homes of the beche-de-mer sailors at Lynn and Wenham, Massachusetts. At little expense, like the worms, it would bring a fabulous profit, even though one-third of it was lost in transit from New England to India. When the **TUSCANY**'s cargo hatch was opened, the native laborers refused to touch the slimy wet cargo— to them it was some kind of evil magic. When they were finally persuaded to carry it piece by piece on their backs to a warehouse, they were further frightened because it lost weight as they walked and sent chills down their spines. To the British in India, however, it was a great novelty and very refreshing in the hot climate. The **TUSCANY**'s cargo was ice. One Indian Parsee asked Captain Littlefield of the **TUSCANY**, *"How does this ice grow in your country, on trees?"*

The unique idea of cutting blocks of ice from New England's frozen ponds in the winter and shipping it to the Tropics came from Bostonian Frederic Tudor. His father and friends thought his idea was outlandish, idiotic and downright crazy. *"The ice will melt in southern waters and your vessel will fill with water and sink,"* said his father. Fred decided to give it a try anyway. He hired men to cut ice blocks weighing from 400 to 500 pounds from a pond in Lynn and drag them by sleigh to the sea to be stacked aboard his ship **FAVORITE**. The 130 tons of ice was then covered with sawdust in the hold of the ship to insulate it, and in February, 1806 the **FAVORITE** headed for the West Indies. After a voyage of almost 2,000 miles, she arrived at Martinique, her cargo still intact— there was very little melting. The only problem was, as it was in India 27 years later, the natives at first refused to touch the misty cargo, and when they finally did, they were shocked that anything in this world could be that cold. The ice was sold for three cents a pound to cool down warm drinks and to help preserve foods. Tudor's venture was a success, and he continued, sending ice to South Carolina, Louisiana and other West Indian ports. Within a few years he was shipping his frozen cargo to Europe, China and Australia, and by 1865, he was delivering ice to 53 ports around the world— in England the queen ordered that Tudor's ice be available at Windsor Castle at all times.

Lorenzo Baker, a successful Yankee trader from Wellfleet, Massachusetts, didn't want anything to do with ice, although unknowing merchants tried to persuade him to use it to preserve his cargoes. His cargo of fortune was what the Moslems called *"the fruit of paradise,"* and unlike most other fruit, if it got too cold, it would be ruined. His accidental introduction to the fruit came in 1870 when he was hired to transport a group of goldminers from New York to a mining camp 200 miles up the Orinoco River in Venezuela. Lorenzo didn't want to head back to New England with an empty ship, so before he left South America he took on a load of bamboo and a couple of bunches of *"something shaped like a dory and that tastes like cooked potatoes only sweeter."* The natives called them bananas. Only one or two of the bananas arrived home in edible condition, but the Wellfleet folks liked the taste. Lorenzo decided to take his schooner **TELEGRAPH** back to South America to get more bananas and some coconuts as well, but this time he would take only green fruit and allow it to ripen during the voyage home. Within two months the **TELEGRAPH** docked at Boston with 1,450 bunches of bananas and 35,000 coconuts. The fruit sold fast, and Baker made a $2,000 profit. He returned to the tropics for more and continued to do so for years, until he became a multi-millionaire — it was the beginning of America's United Fruit Company, which is still going strong today. Lorenzo Baker also saw to it that his *"tropical curiosities,"* each wrapped in tinfoil and selling for ten cents apiece, were the highlight of the 1876 Philadelphia Centennial Exposition. This popularized bananas throughout America, and they were then imported in large quantities. It is unfortunate, however, that bananas weren't discovered and imported to New England some 75 years earlier, for if so, one precious life might have been saved. It is now known that although humans like bananas, no one thrives on them like pachyderms. If *"Old Bet,"* America's first elephant, had been served bananas rather than wine and rum, she might have survived to a ripe old age instead of succumbing to the evils of drink.

Cannibal and King of the Fiji Islands — Thakombau. He liked white meat, and tried to eat the crew of the ***CHARLES DOGGET*** *of Salem. Photo of painting by a seaman courtesy, Peabody Museum, Salem.*

III
WHAT'S IN A NAME?

Men of the sea have always been a superstitious lot — if their vessels avoid mishaps or ride out storms proudly, they are called *"good ships"*; if however, a vessel rolls fretfully in a storm, or seemingly causes accidents and adversities to the captain and the crew, she is forever damned a *"jinxed ship,"* a *"bad ship"* or a *"jonah."*

Ship owners are usually careful in giving their ships a proper, untarnished name, never one that has been connected with tragedy or disaster. You would hardly see a vessel on the high seas today with the name **ANDREA DORIA** or **TITANIC.** When the sloop **GLASGOW** sank off Nantucket Shoal on July 31, 1865, her owners recalled that when the ship was being built, an old Cape Cod fisherman had warned them not to call her **GLASCOW,** for the name was unlucky. One New England schooner named **GLASCOW** had wrecked at Sable Island, Nova Scotia in 1840, and only fourteen years later the **CITY OF GLASGOW** with 400 men, women and children aboard had disappeared in the North Atlantic while on her way to America.

Probably one of the weirdest incidents in nautical history was the discovery of the derelict **MARLBOROUGH-GLASCOW** off the coast of Chile in 1913 by the crew of the British ship **JOHNSON.** They found the derelict drifting close to the jungle shore, *"badly weathered and obscured somewhat by a layer of mossy growth,"* the **JOHNSON** skipper reported to the British Admiralty. Aboard the **M-GLASCOW,** the **JOHNSON** men found a full cargo of lumber and a skeleton crew of 17. The skeletons were still clothed in tattered officers' uniforms and seamen's garb; seven of them were in their bunks in the cabins; three were lying on the bridge; three dressed in uniforms were found at the foot of the companionway; and three more were found huddled under the hatch cover. One skeleton was at the helm, with his bony fingers still on the wheel. After a lengthy investigation by British authorities, it was learned that the **MARLBOROUGH-GLASCOW** had sailed from Littleton, New Zealand on January 8, 1890 with lumber and 24 men aboard. She never made it to her port-of-call; she was thought to have foundered in a storm. No one will ever know what really happened aboard the **M-GLASCOW,** only that she sailed the seas for 23 years with no vessel spotting her until the **JOHNSON** came along.

Vessels are often named after port cities, of course; therefore, the loss of so many **GLASCOW**s might not seem unusual. But there have been vessels names after one particular New England port that have had more than their fair share of bad luck. The freighter **PORTLAND** was torpedoed by a German submarine off the coast of North Carolina on February 11, 1943, and the schooner **PORTLAND** disappeared off Connecticut with her captain and crew on July 16, 1916. Prior to that was the sinking of the steamer **PORTLAND** on May 8, 1884 off the coast of Maine. There is one steamer **PORTLAND**, however, that is still a subject of discussion and debate along the New England coast, even though she sank back in 1898.

On the evening of November 26, 1898 this 281-foot paddlewheeler was tied up at a Boston dock. Over 140 passengers were crowded aboard her, all hoping to be in Portland, Maine by the next morning — Thanksgiving Day. The **PORTLAND**, under the command of Hollis Blanchard, left Boston a few minutes before 7:00 p.m. She actually left port ahead of schedule; in fact, four people who rushed onto the dock at the last minute missed sailing with her, thereby saving their lives.

It was snowing, and the wind was up. At 9:30 p.m. the **PORT-LAND** was seen *"on course off Gloucester"* by a fisherman. At 11:00 p.m. she was spotted from shore, passing Thatcher's Island near Rockport, Massachusetts. These reports indicated that the **PORTLAND** wasn't making much progress, for Gloucester and Rockport are neighboring towns. At 11:30 p.m. the schooner **GRAYLING** was almost capsized by the **PORTLAND** off Thatcher's Island; at midnight she was spotted from shore off Gloucester Harbor. The storm was now forcing the **PORTLAND** backwards. The winds were gusting at 90 miles per hour, and New England was in the middle of a blizzard. At 7:00 the next morning the skipper of the **RUTH M. MARTIN**, also in trouble, spotted the **PORTLAND** off Cape Cod. *"She was drifting with the wind,"* he reported, *"but still under steam."* The **RUTH M. MARTIN** grounded at the tip of Cape Cod a few hours later; the **PORTLAND** was never seen again. At first some people disputed the **MARTIN** skipper's report, for this would mean that the **PORTLAND** had been forced over 100 miles backwards by the wind. The next day, however, a life preserver with **PORTLAND** stamped on it was found on a Cape Cod beach. Then bodies started floating ashore — some were naked or in nightclothes; others were fully dressed in formal clothes, as if they had been attending a dinner party. There were no survivors, and no one knows what caused the ship *"still under steam"* off Cape Cod to sink.

Many vessels are also named after women, usually girlfriends or wives of the vessel owners or skippers. In spite of the good fortune intended, a number of them have run into trouble over the centuries. Ten ships named **EDITH** have disappeared under New England waters over the past 200 years, as have 15 **JENNIE**s, 16 **LIZZIE**s, 13 **MAGGIE**s, 16 **NELLIE**s, 14 EMMAs, 15 **CLARA**s, 22 ANNIEs, 25 **ALICE**s and over 50 **MARY**s. Just within six years, 1858 to 1863, 15 vessels named **ELIZABETH** were wrecked in storms off the New England coast, and nine of them perished in the same area off the tip of Cape Cod. Maybe boat and ship owners should think twice before naming vessels after their favorite gals.

Ships named **ATLANTIC** haven't fared too well either at the mercy of their namesake. The first ships of that name were considered the fastest and were the largest, most luxurious ships afloat in the 1800s. The 1,112-ton super-steamer **ATLANTIC** was the biggest ship on the East Coast in 1846. She travelled Long Island Sound between New York City and ports in Connecticut. Her rival was the steamer **ORE-GON**. In fact, a race between the two ships from Bridgeport to New York had been slated for early December — the **OREGON** captain wagering $5,000 that his ship was faster. The **ATLANTIC**, however, didn't make it into the month of December — her final voyage was on Thanksgiving Day.

She left New London, Connecticut that chilly holiday morning with 118 people aboard headed for the big city. Less than an hour out of port, her steam chest exploded, starting a fire. No one was injured in the explosion, and the fire was quickly extinguished; but helpless without steam power, the **ATLANTIC** started drifting. With a gale wind blowing and the temperature near freezing, she hit the rocks at Fisher's Island stern first. Immediately, a large wave crashed over the women's salon, sweeping it overboard along with six women and five children. The deck was soon caked with ice, and as passengers tried to scramble ashore, many slipped and fell into the icy water. Within five minutes after hitting the rocks, the **ATLANTIC** was shattered to pieces, and 40 people were drowned. Only 29 passengers and 49 crew made it to shore. Of the women and children, only one 12 year old boy, Jacob Watson, survived. All five members of his family had perished. The next day many bodies floated ashore on the Connecticut mainland, along with a carpetbag belonging to the Adams Express Company containing $45,000.

The fastest, plushest ship in the world in 1873 was another luxury liner named **ATLANTIC**. Like the **ATLANTIC** before her, she had a competitor for speed — the French steamer **VILLE-DU-HAVRE**. Although a date for a race between these speedy giants was never set, their captains tried continuously to beat each other's travelling time between Europe and America's East Coast. The 2,366-ton, 420-foot long

ATLANTIC sailed from Liverpool for New York on March 20, 1873. The 976 persons aboard made themselves comfortable as the engineers stuffed the boilers with coal for a swift journey. An Atlantic gale, however, cut down her speed — by March 31 she was six days behind schedule. Because of strong winds and a limited supply of fuel, Captain James Williams headed for the nearer port of Halifax, Nova Scotia rather than New York. It was in the dead of night that Captain Williams spotted the breakers at Mars Head, Mosher Island; however, his discovery came too late to avoid them. The ATLANTIC hit hard at 3:00 a.m., April Fool's Day.

Waves washed over the ship and into the companionways, where many passengers drowned in their bunks. Crewmen got out lines to the rocky shore as some headed for safety in the rigging. A few jumped overboard to take their chances in the freezing water. One steward, Hugh Christie, tried to swim ashore and was only inches away from the rocks and safety when a frightened passenger grabbed him around the neck, and both went under. Some 70 people waited a few hours for the tide to go out and actually walked ashore from the sinking ship; but most who sought safety in the rigging died from exposure. One passenger, a Mr. Burns, remained in his bunk all night with water washing around him. At daylight he walked up on deck, grabbed a lifeline and was pulled to shore. Nova Scotians arrived in boats early in the morning, and those still alive in the rigging were saved by their heroic efforts. Although 546 people died aboard the ATLANTIC, the greatest tragedy of the sinking was that not one woman and only one child, 12 year old John Hinley, survived. One wonders at the coincidence that of all the women and children aboard the two great ATLANTICs, only one 12 year old boy survived each shipwreck.

The macabre story of the 1873 ATLANTIC is not complete without telling what happened to her competitor, the 403-foot steampacket VILLE-DU-HAVRE. She met her end on the evening of November 15, 1873 while she was steaming from New York to France with 313 people aboard, only seven months after the ATLANTIC hit Mosher Island. She was off the Azores when the British ship LOCH EARN plowed into her port side. The VILLE-DU-HAVRE sank within eight minutes, but the much smaller LOCH EARN remained afloat. The British crew immediately put out longboats to search for survivors, but only 87 of the 313 VILLE-DU-HAVRE passengers were saved.

There were many other vessels named ATLANTIC whose careers ended in violent fashion — one a sailing sloop that sank in a storm off

Rockport, Massachusetts in 1829; another a 185-foot sailing yacht that holds a record for sailing the Atlantic from England to America in 12 days, four hours and one minute. The latter now lies off the coast of New Jersey where she sank in a storm on December 5, 1963. Close by her is another **ATLANTIC** that stranded on a sand bar off Seabright, New Jersey in 1921. There are three **ATLANTIC** steamers that sank off the Carolina coast between 1906 and 1925 and another steamer of that name that foundered in Chesapeake Bay in 1876. A freighter **ATLAN-TIC** sank in a hurricane off the Louisiana coast in 1954. The once famous sidewheel steamer **ATLANTIC** plied the waters of Lake Erie in the mid 1800s. She carried over 400 passengers when she collided with the steamer **OGDENSBURG** in a fog on August 19, 1852. Damage to the **OGDENSBURG** was minor, but the **ATLANTIC** sank within minutes, killing 350 passengers — mostly immigrants from Norway.

The British and American Navies, it seems, have also been remiss in naming warships. When a naval vessel sinks, be it in battle or even under peculiar circumstances, the government usually gives another vessel that same name. If she doesn't remain afloat, a third is so honored. For example, there have been many **WASP**s of the United States and British Navies. The first American **WASP**, a Revolutionary War privateer was commissioned by George Washington. She didn't even have a cannon and was manned by only nine crewmen. Her home port was Marblehead, Massachusetts, and her only claim to fame was that she was the smallest ship ever to sail in the American Navy. Little is known about what happened to her, but it's said that when her crew took her fishing she sank in a September storm. The second **WASP**, an 8-gun, 105-foot Revolutionary War schooner was purposely blown up in the Delaware River by her own crew in 1777 to avoid capture by the British. The third **WASP**, launched on April 21, 1806, was an 18-ton sloop of war carrying sailors and marines. When she met up with the British sloop **FROLIC** in the North Atlantic on October 17, 1812, a battle ensued. The vessels were evenly matched in size, cannons and man power. The fighting became so frantic that at one point two of the **WASP**'s cannons got jammed in the **FROLIC**'s bow. When the smoke cleared, the **WASP** had won the day, and the British ensign was struck. On the blood spattered decks of the **FROLIC** 30 men, including the ship's captain, were dead, and 50 were badly wounded. On the **WASP** only 5 were killed and 5 wounded, yet both vessels were badly damaged. As the **WASP**'s commander, Jacob Jones, attempted to escort the **FROLIC** into an East Coast port, the 70-gun British man-of-war **POITIERS** showed up and overtook the **WASP** by firing one shot. She was taken into Bermuda, her captain and crew imprisoned, and the British changed her name to **PEACOCK**. Flying the British ensign, the ex-**WASP** — **PEACOCK** disappeared off the coast of Virginia in a storm in 1813, with all hands lost.

Built in Newburyport, Massachusetts for the War of 1812, the fourth **WASP** of the American Navy sailed for England in 1914 under Commander Blakeley to harass British shipping. Although she captured and sank 13 British merchant ships, the life of this 18-gun, 117-foot **WASP** was less than eight months. She mysteriously disappeared in the Atlantic with her Commander and 173 crewmen in September 1814. There was also a 5-gun sloop **WASP** that sailed Lake Champlain in Thomas Macdonough's fleet during the War of 1812. She was involved in the famous battle at Plattsburg on September 11, 1813 but was scuttled at Whitehall, New York.

The privately owned schooner **WASP** sank in a squall off Gloucester, Massachusetts in September 1849, and the Confederate paddle wheel steamer **WASP** blew up in the Jones River, Virginia in June 1870. The American Navy's steamer-yacht **WASP**, involved in the Spanish American War, ended her days when she caught fire off Pensacola, Florida on June 19, 1919. The brig **WASP** sank in a storm off Clarks Point, Massachusetts on June 12, 1903. Another brig **WASP**, commanded by Edward Perry of Yarmouth, carrying a cargo of lumber to the West Indies in 1839, wrecked off Cawley's Island, Nova Scotia.

The British Navy didn't fare too well with their **WASP**s either. They lost a warship of that name in the 1700s and two **WASP** gunboats in the 1800s. The first gunboat was lost under mysterious circumstances off Tory Island on the West Coast of Ireland on September 15, 1884. At the court martial her sinking was blamed on *"poor navigation"* by her Commander Nicholas. She had drifted off course in a squall, hit the rocks and exploded with only eight of her 58 man crew surviving. The British Admiralty then commissioned another gunboat **WASP** on April 21, 1887. She sailed from England on her way to Shanghai, China but never made her port-of-call. She vanished somewhere off the Philippines on September 15, 1887, three years to the day after the first gunboat **WASP** sank off the coast of Ireland.

Exactly 55 years later, to the day, the American aircraft carrier **WASP**, while on convoy in the Coral Sea, was hit by three torpedoes from the Japanese submarine I-19. Her ammunition dump exploded, and a fire raged out of control. Captain Sherman gave the order to abandon ship, and 1,930 men jumped into the shark infested waters. Most of them were rescued by American destroyers, but 193 either burned to death, drowned or were eaten by sharks, leaving the mighty World War II carrier **WASP** to sink. On September 15, 1942, the day she sank, another aircraft carrier was commissioned into the American Navy, the **U.S.S ORISKANY**. In 1943 the **ORISCANY** was renamed **WASP**, and she fought on during the war to win eight battle stars. On April 26, 1952, however, the carrier **WASP** collided with the U.S. destroyer **HOBSON**, and although the carrier remained afloat, the **HOBSON** sank into the Atlantic, taking 175 sailors down with her. It seems that the month of April was unfortunate for vessels named **WASP**, as was June, when three of them sank. The month of September, however, was truely tragic with seven of the above mentioned 14 **WASP**s ending their days on the high seas in that month. Is this just coincidence, or were all these valiant vessels cursed by the name bestowed upon them — **WASP**, that stinging insect tha usually dies in September when the cold sets in?

While I was putting along in Salem Harbor with my brother Jim one breezy afternoon in September 1981 aboard the Harbor Master's boat **BOWDITCH**, a call came over the marine radio that the yacht **SEABIRD** was in distress off Gloucester. My brother, the Salem Harbor Master, headed the **BOWDITCH** out to sea to assist in the rescue of the **SEABIRD**. Meanwhile, I wondered how anyone could name a vessel **SEABIRD** with the rivers, lakes and sea bottoms of America so replete with sunken ships of that name.

There had been the sailing ship **SEABIRD** that sank off Gloucester in 1878, and the steamer **SEABIRD** that burned and sank at Waukegan, Illinois ten years before that with 72 lives lost. Six years earlier, the Confederate steamer **SEABIRD** was sunk by Union ships in North Carolina's Pasquotank River, and in 1848 another steamer of that name burned and sank at Cape Girardeau, Missouri. There was another steamer **SEABIRD** which sank in Lake Michigan in 1886. The most recent **SEABIRD** tragedy was that of a steamer-packet that caught fire and burned to the water-line in New York's East River on May 9, 1932.

New England's first **SEABIRD**, however, was a true mystery ship. She came crashing ashore under full sail at Newport, Rhode Island on a stormy October day in 1850. When she slid onto Eastern Beach, villagers boarded her and found the ship to be in order, but there was no crew. The only living thing aboard was a dog. The **SEABIRD** had been sailing from Honduras under the command of Rhode Island's John Huxham when, for some unknown reason, Huxham and his crew had disappeared never to be seen again. To add to the mystery, two days after the **SEABIRD** had beached herself at Newport, she too disappeared. Whether she drifted off or was taken back out to sea by unknown sailors no one knows, for she was never seen again; and the only article left behind on the beach was the mongrel dog.

When the yacht **SEABIRD** and her crew were safely brought into Gloucester Harbor on that breezy September day in 1981, I was tempted to suggest to the yachtsman that he change the name of his ship. I didn't because I thought he would think I was overly superstitious. Maybe I am, but how do you explain away the loss of so many vessels with the same name — especially when it's a nice, nonaggressive name like **SEABIRD** or like . . . **FRIENDSHIP**?

On August 31, 1954 the oil tanker **FRIENDSHIP** foundered and sank into deep water at No Man's Land off the Massachusetts coast. Almost 100 years earlier the 36-ton schooner **FRIENDSHIP** was driven ashore and sank at Tusket Island in Nova Scotia waters near the coast of Maine. Nearby, another schooner **FRIENDSHIP** crashed into the South Breakers off Hichens Cove at Seal Island on June 26, 1832. Seal Island is located off Yarmouth near the watery border line between Maine and Nova Scotia. On January 17, 1817, less than 15 years earlier, a brig crashed ashore at South Breakers, Hichens Cove, Seal Island — the very spot where the schooner **FRIENDSHIP** sank — and her name was **FRIENDSHIP**.

At Montauk, Connecticut in August 1839 a schooner washed ashore which set brother against brother, neighbor against neighbor, nation against nation, President against President, and finally America against herself. The derelict schooner **AMISTAD** was filled with 44 African slaves. They had slain the schooner's captain and forced the crew to abandon ship; however, in trying to redirect the schooner back to Africa from Cuba, they ended up in Connecticut — then in jail. The blacks were put on trial for mutiny and piracy in New Haven in January 1840. The pro-slavers battled the growing anti-slavery groups in court, with President Van Buren openly taking one side and former President of the United States, John Quincy Adams, showing up in the New Haven District Court to take the Africans' side. Spain pressured Van Buren to give up the slaves to Cuba, so he sent the naval brig **GRAMPUS** to Connecticut to deliver them to Havana, even though the Connecticut District Court declared that the slaves were free to return to Africa. The **AMISTAD**'s human cargo created quite a stir in America and was certainly a factor leading up to the Civil War some 22 years later. It's a strange twist of fate that the slave ship **AMISTAD** should become the symbol of emancipation in New England, and even more remarkable for those who understand Spanish, for **AMISTAD** in Spanish means **FRIENDSHIP**. She obviously didn't live up to her name. Ask any old New England sailor, and he'll tell you much more about what's in a name, and he will also warn you never to set foot on a ship named **GLASCOW, PORTLAND, MARY, ELIZABETH, ATLANTIC, WASP, SEABIRD** or **FRIENDSHIP**.

The luxury liner ATLANTIC wrecks off Mosher Island, Nova Scotia on April 1, 1873, and the steamer PORTLAND sinks off Cape Cod on November 26, 1898. Sketch and photo courtesy The Peabody Museum, Salem, MA.

IV
FLOTSAM AND JETSAM

The **H. M. S. ATLANTA** was a 923-ton, 131-foot long training frigate for British sailors. She sailed from Portsmouth, England on November 7, 1879 with 290 officers and crew aboard. After stopping at Bermuda to drop off four sick sailors, she sailed for the West Indies on April 4, 1880 and was never seen again. In May of that year, the British government offered $2,000 for any information regarding her whereabouts; a month later a clue did turn up. On June 14, Edward Millet, while fishing one mile off the coast of Rockport, Massachusetts found a bottle drifting with the current. Inside the bottle was a message. It read: *"April 17, 1880 — training ship ATLANTA. We are sinking in L. 270°, Lat. 32° — Any person finding this note will please advertise in the daily papers — John L. Hutchins. Distress."*

The position Mr. Hutchins gives in his note is south of the Azores, which would mean the **ATLANTA** had drifted considerably off her course, or more probably was forced off course by an Atlantic storm. Two days after fisherman Millet found the note in the bottle, children playing on the beach at Cow Bay, Halifax, Nova Scotia found a barrel stave in the sand. On this sea-soaked piece of wood, written in pencil was a message that read: *"ATLANTA going down. April 15, 1880. No hope. Send this to Mrs. Mary White, Sussex — James White."* These messages were the only items ever found from the ill-fated frigate.

There have been many intriguing incidents in the sea regarding flotsam and jetsam, especially in the form of bottles with notes in them. Probably the most unique of these occurred on a beach in Japan in 1935. While digging in the sand near the water s edge at Hiratamura, a boy found an old bottle containing a note of distress. Realizing its importance but not fully understanding the message in the bottle, the boy rushed to a nearby police station. The police chief read the note and didn't know whether to laugh or cry. The note gave the location of a shipwreck. The man who wrote it said that he was the only survivor of 46 sailors who had sailed on a ship that was wrecked on an island. He was awaiting rescue. The policeman, with finder's permission, turned the note and bottle over to the Tokyo Museum where it was placed on display for all to see. The note in the bottle was dated *"June 17, 1784."*

On December 4, 1853 a small lead tube was found under six inches of sand on the banks of the Missisquoi River near Swanton, Vermont.

Orlando Green had uncovered it while digging sand for a local marble mill. Inside the four inch tube was a rolled up piece of coarse brown paper, and on it in bold, irregular script was a message — a message that shocked American geographers and historians. The note read: *"This is the solme daye. I must now die. This is the 90th day since we lef the ship. All have perished and on the banks of this river I die too, so farewelle, may future posteritye knowe our end — John Graye."* Experts studied the paper and the writing, both were deemed authentic — although English, the writing resembled a form of 16th century Dutch. The shocker was that the note was dated *"November 29 AD 1564."* It was on the morning of July 4, 1609 that famous explorer Samuel de Champlain and his companions *"glided silently into the waters of that beautiful lake which hence-forth was to bear his name,"* Edward Collins tells us in his *History of Vermont* — no white man had been there before him. The message in the tube, however, reveals that Champlain wasn't the first European into Vermont — nor did he discover Lake Champlain — John Gray and his shipmates were there 45 years before him.

Less than three years before Orlando Green found the controversial note in a lead tube, another tragic note was discovered in Hingham Harbor on Boston's South Shore — it had been in the water inside a bottle for only two days. The Hingham Historical Society presently has the note and bottle on display. The note reads: *"Wednesday night April 16 — the lighthouse won't stand over tonight. She shakes two feet each way now — J.W. and J.A."* Joseph Wilson and Joseph Antonio were two young men who had volunteered to be assistant lighthouse keepers at Minot's Light, Cohasset, Massachusetts. The head lighthouse keeper was a Mr. Bennett, but on that fateful April day he was on the mainland buying a boat. Minot's Light, a spidery looking structure 75 feet high, was built in 1849 on a small platform of rocks some three miles offshore. The previous keeper, a Mr. Dunham, had quit his duties, believing that the lighthouse was unsafe in storms.

On the night of April 16, 1851 as a storm whipped the New England coast, the lighthouse started to sway. Waves splashed over the structure, but the two Joes kept the light burning. People of the mainland said that they could hear the lighthouse bell ringing until after midnight, but then there was just the howling of the wind. The lighthouse toppled into the sea, and the two assistant keepers were found the next morning floating dead on the surface near shore. They had dispensed the note in the bottle only a few hours before the lighthouse toppled.

A warm autumn day in 1847 started out being the happiest day in

Susan Hichborn's life. Late morning, she and 24 others boarded her father's schooner **SUSAN** at Rockport, Massachusetts. They were all travelling some 25 miles by sea to Boston where Susan Hichborn was to be married. Rounding Cape Ann, the **SUSAN** met a storm. At a pier in Boston Harbor, Susan's fiance waited the entire day, but the schooner carrying his bride-to-be and the wedding party never showed up. That evening a trunk floated into Boston Harbor; the man who recovered it from the water was Susan's fiance. Etched into the side of the trunk were the initials S.H., and inside the trunk was Susan's wedding gown. No wreckage or bodies from the **SUSAN** were ever found.

An even more startling story of flotsam is that of Charles Coghlan, the famous 19th century actor. He was born in France but bred at Prince Edward Island, Nova Scotia. He later disappointed his parents when, after they had paid dearly to educate him in England, he decided against their wishes to become an actor. Charles, however, was exceptional on the stage. One of his understudies was later to become the great movie actor Monty Wooley. Before Charles Coghlan became famous, British actress Lily Langtree reports, he went to a fortune teller who told him that although he would become rich and famous, he would die at the height of his fame in a southern American city. She also said that he would not rest in peace until he returned to his childhood home. Coghlan jokingly retold this strange prediction to his friends, including Monty Wooley and Lily Langtree, many times.

Playing the role of Hamlet to a packed audience in Galveston, Texas on November 27, 1899, Charles Coghlan dropped dead. He was buried at the seaside cemetery in Galveston. A hurricane hit the Gulf of Mexico on September 8, 1900 which washed away a portion of the Galveston waterfront, including the cemetery and Coghlan's grave. Eight years later, on October 16, an oblong box identified by a silver plate as the coffin of Charles Coghlan, was found floating in Fortune Bay at Prince Edward Island by two fishermen. Charles Coghlan in his coffin had apparently drifted almost 3,000 miles with the Gulf Stream to his old Nova Scotian home. He now supposedly rests in the cemetery at Prince Edward Island. This incredible, almost unbelievable tale of a coffin transporting itself through the Gulf of Mexico and up the East Coast of America to Nova Scotia has been criticized as a hoax by some writers, but supported and repeated by others, including Robert Ripley and William Wisner. Actually, flotsam and jetsam drifting with the Gulf Stream up the East Coast from the tropics to New England and sometimes beyond is not unusual, and floating coffins have often been found drifting at sea.

In the 1890s the Gloucester schooner **BELVIDERE**, Captain Samuel Elwell commanding, came upon a small oblong box floating in the waters off George's Bank. The fishermen hauled it aboard, and, forcing open the lid, found the decomposing body of a 4 year old girl inside. Elwell had his crewmen cut holes into the bottom of the box, which was obviously a coffin, and he dropped it back into the sea to sink. Who the child was, and why the coffin was drifting at George's Bank, far out to sea, no one knows.

Off the coast of Gloucester in the summer of 1972 an old seaman was buried at sea with full funeral ceremony, but three weeks after the burial, in his weighted coffin he was found drifting further out to sea on the surface waters. The coffin was towed in by the crew of the fishing boat who discovered it, a few more rocks were added to the box, and the seaman was deposited back into the depths, this time — hopefully — for good.

There are three miraculous incidents in New England history, when live little human beings, all female, were discovered amidst the flotsam and jetsam spewed up from the sea. In March of 1883 the coastal schooner **HELEN AND MARY**, carrying a cargo of granite, was sailing from Halifax to Boston when a storm capsized the vessel near Mount Desert Island, Maine. The heavy cargo caused the **HELEN AND MARY** to sink immediately. Only one man, first mate Nelson White, managed to remain afloat clinging to the wreckage. As air bubbles escaped from the schooner, an oilskin jacket popped to the surface. The jacket ws bouyed by air trapped inside it, and Nelson grabbed for it, hoping to use it as a life preserver. Inside the jacket, however, was something solid — a baby, less than a year old and not even wet. The baby was Nelson White's neice, daughter of the ship's captain, Jared Parker and White's sister Helen, who had both gone down with the schooner. Although White's fingers were numbed with cold, he managed to strap the child to his chest with a cord. He then floated for some two hours in the frigid water until crewmen aboard the ship **IRIS** spotted him and his bundle drifting with the currents some ten miles off the coast. Nelson White was almost unconscious from the cold, but he revived without any lasting effects, and the child also survived the long cold bath without any problems — they later both returned to Halifax.

Also in March ten years earlier, at the mouth of Maine's Sheepscat River, a violent storm drove a schooner onto the shoals in sight of the Hendrick's Head Lighthouse. The lighthouse keeper saw the vessel hit and start to break apart, but the sea was too rough for him to venture out in his boat in an attempt to save lives. He was helpless and frustrated to tears as he watched the unknown schooner slowly sink only a few hundred yards away. When wreckage began floating in on the breakers, he ventured out into the shallows hoping beyond hope that a person might be clinging to it. Two items he managed to snag and pull ashore were feather sleeping pads lashed together with rope. He cut the rope and found a small box wrapped in blankets wedged between the two pads. Inside the box was a wriggling baby girl, the only survivor of the shipwreck. He rushed her back to the lighthouse to warm her by the stove. That lighthouse became her home for the next 18 years. Neither her name nor the name of the schooner were ever known.

The schooner **POLLY** out of Provincetown, Massachusetts, Captain Ned Rider commanding, fished the waters off Cape Breton, Nova Scotia every year from the turn of the 19th century well into the 1820s. In 1803 the captain's 10 year old nephew, Peter Rider, joined the crew of the **POLLY** on their autumn fishing voyage. One day, anchored off a small outcropping of rocks near Saint Paul Island, Nova Scotia, Peter thought he heard a child's cries coming from amongst the rocks. The captain insisted it was only the screech of seagulls, but young Peter wanted to investigate. Taking the schooner tender, he rowed to the rocks where, standing in waist deep water with bits of wreckage floating about her, was a little girl about 3 years old. Peter rowed the sobbing child back to the **POLLY**. Although she was asked many times where she came from and who she was, her only response was to cry. Saint Paul Island was uninhabited, so Captain Rider knew she hadn't come from there. It was assumed she was shipwrecked and washed onto the rocks — apparently the only survivor. She was brought back to Provincetown to live with the Riders. When Ned Rider died some ten years later, Peter Rider took over command of the **POLLY**. He twice interrupted his fishing voyages to stop at Cape Breton, attempting to discover who the little girl was and how she had become marooned on the rocky reef; but he got no answers. Ruth Rider, as she was called, was married in Provincetown in 1816 to Peter Rider, the boy who had saved her — their descendants reside in Provincetown to this day.

In March 1982 a woman found a bottle with a note in it at a beach on Nantucket Island. The note was from the owner of a Miami, Florida hotel offering the finder a seven-day, all expenses paid vacation at the hotel. The only problem was that the written offer was dated 1964. The hotel was contacted, and although the original owner had long since sold his interest in the hotel, the new owner honored the 18 year old promotion gimmick. Exactly 100 bottles with similar free vacation offers had been tossed into Miami waters at the same time, but the Nantucket woman was the first one to claim her prize. There are still 99 bottles out there somewhere, drifting along in the Gulf Stream. *"We are more than happy to have her stay with us,"* said the hotel owner, *"but we expected her much earlier."*

In April 1976 Lester Willis of Miami, Florida scribbled a note on a piece of paper, dropped it inside a bottle and, just for fun, dropped it into Biscayne Bay. July 29th of that same year, Tom Daily of Boston was fishing from the motor-yacht **HUSTLER** off Falmouth, Massachusetts, when he snagged a 200-pound shark. *"In the belly of the shark,"* Daily informed Willis, *"while cleaning out its innards, I was amazed to find your bottle and letter."*

Finding bottles drifting with notes in them, arriving from the Deep South to New England within a few months, is not a recent occurrence. In fact the Gulf Stream was discovered in the mid-18th century by Boston born Ben Franklin in this manner.

After studying the currents of the Gulf Stream, the entire fifth grade class at Falmouth, Massachusetts deposited some 20 Coke bottles with letters in them at Newfoundland, hoping to discover where the currents flowed once they left the East Coast. Each letter asked the finder to write and tell them where the bottle was found. They dated their letters on the day they were sent adrift, August 14, 1982. Less than four months later, 11 year old Julie Chereau of Falmouth received a letter from 14 year old Gilles Devallon of Agen, France. He had found her bottle with the note in it on an Agen Beach in early December. The Mayor of Agen also wrote a letter to the Selectmen of Falmouth, asking about the Cape Cod town and what it was like to live there. The Selectmen wrote back, answering the Mayor's questions and inquiring about his town. The publishers of two French newspapers then financed an all expenses paid trip to America for the Devallon family. The French family arrived in Falmouth in August 1983, exactly one year after Julie had set her bottle adrift. Many residents of the Cape Cod town turned out to greet them, showering Gilles with gifts. Julie Chereau then visited Agen, France. A wonderful friendship between two children, two families and two towns separated by the Atlantic Ocean has developed because of a bit of flotsam carried by the currents. Perhaps one of the children's bottles will drift to Russia, and the town of Falmouth can then teach our leaders in Washington, D.C. an elementary lesson in successful international relations.

Another lesson for all of us is never to pass up an empty bottle floating at sea or lying on the beach, for it might have a note in it that could change your life for the better. Many a romance and even marriage has resulted between the senders and finders of bottles with notes in them. In fact, in the case of Jack Wurm of San Francisco, a fortune resulted. In the bottle he found on a California beach in March 1949 was a note that read: *"I leave my entire estate to the lucky person who finds this bottle — Daisy Alexander June 20, 1937."* She gave her address as London, England. Daisy had dropped the bottle, with her will in it, into the Thames River, and in less than twelve years it had floated down the river into the Atlantic, and some how made it into the Pacific Ocean. It was no hoax or joke; Daisy *"Singer"* Alexander was a wealthy eccentric who died in the early 1940s leaving no will. Jack Wurm received over $6,000,000 plus Daisy's valuable stock in the Singer Sewing Machine Company. What does multimillionaire, former beach comber Jack Wurm have to say about his fabulous find? *"As the Good Book says, 'there's a time to sew and there's a time to reap.'"*

A storm at Minot's Light, Cohasset — the previous lighthouse toppled in 1851, killing two boys.

V
NEVER EAT A NEW ENGLANDER

The galley **NOTTINGHAM** of London — after taking on a cargo of cordage, butter and cheese at Ireland — sailed for Boston on September 25, 1710. She was a seaworthy ship of 120 tons, carrying ten guns and fourteen men, but for 16 straight days she was buffeted by wind and wave. Freezing rain and snow, whipped up by a northeast gale, added to the misery aboard the **NOTTINGHAM**. Then it hailed for two days, forcing everyone but the helmsman below decks. *"Thereafter, we had no observation for ten to twelve days,"* said the **NOTTINGHAM**'s captain, John Dean.

In the dead of night the lookout shouted *"breakers ahead !"* and Captain Dean rushed forward to see great waves spewing white foam over an outcropping of rocks. The **NOTTINGHAM** struck the east end of Boon Island Ledge — a 100 yard by 50 yard slab of craggy rocks some fifteen miles off the coast of Maine. The breakers heaved the ship alongside the rocks where she started breaking up. *"We, however, went upon deck,"* said Captain Dean, *"and the force of the sea soon broke the masts, so they fell right towards the shore."* Dean ordered his men to crawl to the tip of the downed masts in an attempt to make the rocks.

"The rocks were extremely slippery and I could not get hold," said Dean. *"I tore my fingers, hands, and arms in the most deplorable manner, every wash of the sea fetching me off again, so that it was with the utmost peril and difficulty that I got safe on shore at last."*

Dean, although wet and frozen, was heartened by the discovery that all of his 13 men had survived the shipwreck. Their troubles, however, were just beginning. *"We endeavored to gain shelter to the leeward of the rocks,"* said Dean, *"but found it so small and inconsiderable that it would afford none, and so very craggy that we could not walk to keep ourselves warm, the weather still continuing extremely cold, with snow and rain."*

As dawn approached, the men started scouring the rocks, hoping that some of their cheese and butter cargo had washed ashore, but only three small pieces of cheese were found, and when divided, were but a mouthful per man. Pieces of the masts and yards, cables, old canvas, and some timber were collected from the rocks which were used to construct a makeshift tent. They had no flint, but tried every means to get a fire started. Their efforts, however, were in vain — everything was water soaked. They gathered some sea moss, kelp and a few shellfish to eat that day; and at night, they cuddled together under the canvas as close to each other as possible for warmth.

Next day, the weather had cleared somewhat and they could see the grey woods and hills of the mainland. Before noon that day, the cook died. *"We laid him in a convenient place for the sea to carry him away,"* said Dean. *"None mentioned eating him, though several, with myself, afterwards acknowledged that they had thoughts of it."*

Their third night on Boon Island was the most miserable with a bad frost and extreme cold that numbed their hands and feet almost useless. Some of the men pulled off their boots, desiring to wrap their feet in oakum or canvas, but their feet were so cold and blistered that *"in getting off our stockings, we pulled off skin and all, and some, the nails off their toes."*

To further dampen their spirits, three boats were spotted by the men later that day sailing about ten miles off the island — the men shouted together until their throats were raw; they waved their shirts and canvas, but they were neither heard nor seen. *"We were now reduced to the most melancholy and deplorable situation imaginable,"* said Dean. *"Almost every man was weak to an extremity, nearly starved with hunger and perishing with cold, with large and deep ulcers in their legs, the smell of which was highly offensive... and we had nothing to support our feeble bodies but rockweed and a few muscles, scarce and difficult to be procured, at most not above two or three for each man a day... To aggravate our situation, if possible, we had reason to apprehend, lest the approaching spring tide, if accompanied with high winds, should entirely overflow us. The horrors of such a situation it is impossible to describe."*

On Christmas day *"as a slight alleviation of our faith,"* Providence delivered a sea gull to fly so low over the island that the first mate was able to down it with a rock. Dean divided the scrawny bird into equal portions, and although scarcely affording a mouthful for each, they ate the tough raw meat thankfully. Dean then proposed that they attempt to build a raft. *"this proposal was strongly supported by a Swede, one of our men, a stout brave fellow,"* said Dean, *"who had lost the use of both his feet by the frost."*

Within two days they had built a four foot raft from the wreckage on the island, and out of two hammocks that had washed ashore, they made a sail. Two men, one the Swede, *"got upon the raft, but a swell, rolling very high, soon overset them. The Swede not daunted by this accident, swam on shore, but the other, being no swimmer, continued some time* underwater; as soon as he appeared, I caught hold of him and saved him."

The Swede insisted on mounting the raft again and another of the crew joined him. This time they managed to sail away. *"I watched them,"* said Dean, *"and by sunset judged them to be half way to the mainland."* But the Swede and his mate did not make it — they were never seen again.

Two days later, a large piece of green hide fastened to a piece of timber washed onto the rocks. Dean carried it to the tent where the men minced it into small pieces and ate it.

On the last day of December, the fat carpenter died. *"Fastening a rope to the body,"* said Dean, *"with some difficulty, we dragged it out of the tent. But fatigue so overcame my spirits, that being ready to faint, I crept into the tent and was no sooner there than to add to my trouble, the men began to request my permission to eat the dead body, the better to support their lives."*

Dean, a deeply religious man, thought for many hours on the subject. *"After mature consideration of the lawlessness or sinfulness on the one hand, and absolute necessity on the other, judgement and conscience were obliged to submit to the more prevailing arguments of our craving appetites."*

Dean first ordered his men to cut off the carpenter's skin, head, hands and feet and to bury them at sea. The body was then quartered and hung to dry for a few hours. Then Dean cut the flesh into thin slices and washed them in salt water. At first, three of the men refused to eat, but by the next morning, they had joined the others of the **NOTTINGHAM** crew in cannibalism.

"I found that they all ate with the utmost avidity," said Dean, *"but in a few days, I found their dispositions entirely changed, and that affectionate, peaceable temper they had hitherto manifested, totally lost. Their eyes looked wild and staring, their countenances fierce and barbarous. Instead of obeying my commands as they had universally and cheerfully done before, I now found even prayers and entreaties vain and fruitless; nothing was now to be heard but brutal quarrels with horrid oaths . . ."*

Dean kept a continuous watch over what remained of the body of the carpenter, fearing some of his men might try to steal more than their equal share, and knowing that when this food was gone, they might be compelled to feed upon the living.

On the morning of January 2, 1711 as Dean was creeping out of the tent, he saw a small sail boat about half way from shore heading towards the island. Dean called to the others, and all who could stand waved the boat on. Two men in the boat dropped anchor about 50 yards off shore, sea swells preventing them from approaching nearer. Dean shouted to them and pleaded that they try to make a landing and bring something to make a fire. At noon, when the waters were calmer, one of the men climbed into a small canoe that was aboard the boat, and he paddled to the rocks.

"After helping him up with his canoe," said Dean, *"and seeing nothing to eat, I asked him if he could give us fire. He answered in the affirmative, but was so affrighted by our thin and meagre appearance that, at first, he could scarcely return me an answer."*

Dean returned to the tent to show the man the deplorable condition of his many sick crewmen, and they managed to light a campfire which lifted their spirits. Dean then boarded the canoe with the man, *"but the sea immediately drove us against the rock with such violence that we were overset, and being very weak, it was considerable time before I could recover myself, so that I had again a very narrow escape from drowning. The good man, with great difficulty,"* said Dean, *"got on board the shallop without me, designing to return the next day with better conveniences, if the weather should permit."*

The weather, however, immediately worsened— the wind blowing hard from the southeast — and almost swamped the shallop as it returned to the mainland. The next day continued stormy and the **NOTTINGHAM** crew, huddled in their makeshift tent, were in poor spirits. *"Our situation was extremely miserable,"* said Dean. *"We, however, received great benefit from our fire, as we could both warm ourselves and broil our meat."*

The storm continued through the following day *"and the men being very importunate for flesh, I gave them rather more than usual,"* said Dean, *"but not to their satisfaction. They certainly would have eaten up the whole at once had I not carefully watched them with the intention of sharing the rest next morning, if the weather continued bad."*

The wind abated that evening, and in the morning a shallop was anchored off the island. A Mr. Long, Captain Purver and three others from the mainland paddled a large canoe ashore. They brought bread and rum with them, but made the victims eat and drink sparingly. *"After we tasted warm, nourishing food,"* said Dean, *"we became so exceeding hungry and ravenous that had not our friends dieted us and limited the quantity, we should certainly have destroyed ourselves with eating.''*

Within two hours they were aboard the shallop and taken to Piscataqua, Maine. None of the **NOTTINGHAM** crew ever completely recovered the full use of their hands and feet, and some suffered the amputation of toes and fingers. The only one who recovered fully to return to a life on the sea was Captain John Dean.

Exactly 55 years later, the brigantine **PEGGY** out of New York was on a routine voyage, dropping off cargo at the Azores and picking up wine and brandy for her return trip to home port. The commander of the vessel was David Harrison, originally from Gloucester, Massachusetts. The only other New Englanders aboard were David Flatt of Boston, crewman, and Marco, a black man, who was the captain's servant. The 14 other crewmen were a mixed bag of Americans, Englishmen, Welchmen, Frenchmen and a Swede.

The **PEGGY** ran into a violent storm on October 26, 1765 and another on November 1, causing her great damage; her masts toppled and her sails were torn to rags. She was driven off course, and throughout November she drifted helplessly at the mercy of wind and wave. To make matters worse, by December 1st the captain and crew ran out of provisions and were forced to break open the cargo to subsist on a liquid diet. Their only water supply was in two gallon jugs, kept by the captain in his cabin. The captain remained in his cabin too weak to move, suffering from a severe attack of the gout. Many members of the crew tried to appease their hunger by remaining intoxicated for days.

On December 15th a vessel was spotted, and the **PEGGY** crew sent up distress signals. The schooner sailed in and her crew trimmed sails to get within hailing distance of the derelict and her emaciated crew. David Flatt shouted to the captain of the schooner that they were starving, in need of food and water, and a tow to the nearest port. The captain of the unknown schooner nodded as if understanding their dilemma, ordered his crew to crowd on all sail, and either out of cruelty, or thinking the **PEGGY** crew were pirates, sailed away, leaving them in their misery. The starving and thirsty crewmen were enraged, then overcome with despair. They decided to kill and eat Captain Harrison's three pets, two pigeons and a cat, which he brought aboard with him on all voyages. Feeling somewhat remorseful after dividing the meat between them, the crew offered the head of the cat to the captain. *"However disgusting it would have been on any other occassion,"* the captain later reported, *"at that moment, it was a treat, exquisitely delicious."*

For Christmas dinner, the crew ate candles and bits of leather, but by New Year's Day, 1766, there was nothing left on board to sink their teeth into. That day, the crew unanimously decided to sacrifice one of their own to save the lives of the others. They went to Captain Harrison's cabin to tell him of their decision. He was against it, calling it *"an atrocious crime,"* but the first mate said he didn't care if the captain approved or not for they would do it anyway.

The men returned to the deck to draw lots, and Marco, the captain's servant, the only black man aboard the **PEGGY**, lost the draw. There was no doubt in the captain's mind that the first mate had fixed the lottery, but Marco was immediately hit over the head with a hammer, his throat was cut, and he was dismembered piece by piece to be cooked in a pot on deck. One crewman who couldn't wait for the deck fire to bring the pot to a boil, tore out Marco's liver and ate it raw. He soon went into convulsions, became a raving lunatic and died. The crew at first decided to eat him too, but then rejected the idea because he was insane when he died, and the meat might be tainted, driving them out of their minds as well — so they threw him overboard. The only one who refused to eat any part of Marco was Captain Harrison, who was subsisting on brandy and water.

By mid January the famished crew was ready to hold a second lottery. This time the captain consented and decided to run it himself, after the first one resulted in the suspicious loss of his servant. He wrote the name of each crewmember on a small folded piece of paper and deposited the names into a hat. The first mate, with trembling fingers, drew the name of the victim — it was David Flatt. *"The only thing I request of you all,"* he said to the crew, resigned to his fate, *"is not to keep me long in pain. Dispatch me as speedily as you did the negro."* He turned to the Swede who delivered the mortal blow to Marco. The Swede wept, as did some of the other crewmembers. Flatt, still in his late teens, was the youngest among them. Flatt asked for one hour to prepare himself for death, but Captain Harrison prevailed on the unhappy crew to wait until the next morning to do him in. Although Flatt obviously didn't want to die and be eaten, he begged them not to wait until morning, but the captain insisted on the delay.

At 10:00 a.m. on the morning of January 20th, a large fire was prepared on deck to cook David Flatt. He was feverish and so weak that two crewmen had to assist him to the rail, where he requested he be looking out to sea when the fatal blow came. Standing there, a final prayer on his lips, he saw a sail on the horizon. At first he thought his eyes were playing tricks and that the vessel was but wishful thinking, but then the others saw it too. It was the bark **SUSAN** from Virginia, on her way to

England. Spying the derelict, the **SUSAN**'s captain sailed in close. A boat was then lowered and rowed over to the **PEGGY**, loaded with food and water. David Flatt was so elated that he fainted. The **SUSAN** took the **PEGGY** in tow to London, and on the way, two of the **PEGGY** crewmen died, but all the others recovered, including David Flatt, who gave up his life on the sea and became a farmer. Captain Harrison continued on commanding cargo vessels, but carried extra provisions and a fat cat with him on every subsequent voyage.

Again, exactly 55 years passed before that hideous word *"cannibalism"* was whispered through the streets of every New England village and town. This time it wasn't Englishmen marooned on a rock, nor foreigners ready to devour one of our sturdy New England boys, it was New Englanders eating other New Englanders.

The 260-ton whalingship **ESSEX** sailed from Nantucket on August 19, 1819, bound for the South Seas, Captain George Pollard commanding, with a crew of 19. On November 20, 1820 they were south of the Equator in the mid-Pacific, thousands of miles from the nearest land, with 800 barrels of whale oil aboard — it was already a profitable voyage. Another school of whales was spotted that day, and three 30-foot long whale boats were launched from the **ESSEX** to pursue them. Harpooning one enormous sperm whale, First Mate Owen Chase's whaleboat was damaged by the wounded beast, and he was forced to return to the mother ship without his catch. It was that same wounded whale, Owen Chase concluded, that attacked the **ESSEX**. *"He came down upon us with full speed,"* Chase later wrote, *"and struck the ship with his head, just forward of the forechains; he gave us such an appalling and tremendous jar as nearly threw us on our faces."* The **ESSEX** heeled over and fell on her beam ends, stove in and slowly sinking. Captain Pollard had the men cut away the masts, and the **ESSEX** righted herself again. But the hull was badly damaged and only empty casks in the hold were keeping her afloat temporarily. Then the wounded whale surfaced again, *"about one hundred rods to leeward,"* said Chase, *"apparently in convulsions, leaping some twenty feet out of the water and snapping its enormous jaw."* It attacked the ship again, using its head as a battering ram. *"The ship was brought up as suddenly and violently as if she had struck a rock,"* said Chase, *"and she trembled for a few minutes like a leaf."* Captain Pollard ordered the men to rescue as much food, water, tools and navigation instruments as possible before the ship went under. The crew was dumb-founded — *"We looked at each other with perfect amazement, deprived almost of the power of speech,"* Chase later recalled. *"We* *were dejected by this sudden, most mysterious and overwhelming calamity— we were more than a thousand miles from the nearest land, with nothing but three light open boats."*

From the flooding hold the crew managed to salvage 600 pounds of biscuits, 200 gallons of water, two compasses, two quadrants and two live turtles that they had captured weeks earlier at the Galapagos Islands and managed to keep alive by setting them on their backs. They also recovered tools and nails plus three of the ship's spars and some canvas which they used to rig sails on the whaleboats. At noon on November 22, the three little boats sailed away from the doomed derelict, seven men in each of two boats and six in the third, including two cabin boys, Owen Coffin and Thomas Nicholson. Captain Pollard was in charge of one boat, Owen Chase another, and Second Mate Matthew Joy, the third. They headed south southeast toward the coast of South America, over 3,000 miles away.

The food was rationed, one biscuit per day per man, and one half pint of water per day per man. On November 30th the turtles were killed and the meat cooked in their shells. They also ate flying fish that occasionally bumped into the sails, and they drank their own urine. *"The violence of a raging thirst has no parallel in the catalogue of human calamities,"* said Owen Chase.

On December 20th they spotted land, a lone uninhabited island, now known as Henderson Island. It is located only three days sail from Pitcairn Island, where the **BOUNTY** mutineers had found asylum and set up camp in 1792, and where their Polynesian families still lived, but the **ESSEX** victims didn't know this. Landing at Henderson Island, the 18 men and two boys found a fresh water stream and birds to eat. They also found a cave with human skeletons in it, and a nearby tree with the name *"Elizabeth"* carved into the bark — either the name of a girlfiend or wife, but probably the name of a ship that the men in the cave once sailed in. On the day after Christmas, Captain Pollard decided it was time to sail on to the coast of Chile or Peru, for the island could not sustain all their needs for any length of time. Crewmen Thames Chappell, William Wright and Seth Weeks, however, opted to stay on the island rather than continue the uncomfortable journey in an open boat. Captain Pollard agreed to let them stay, promising to send back help once he reached the mainland.

On the day after the three boats left the island, Second Mate Matthew Joy died, and he was dropped overboard, Third Mate Obed Hendricks taking command of his boat. A day later, January 10, 1821, a violent storm separated the three boats, and from that day on, things became even more desperate in each of the three boats. In Chase's boat, crewman Richard Peterson was caught stealing a biscuit and became so repentant that he refused to eat again— he died on January 20th, and his body was deposited over the side. Isaac Cole went mad and tore the leather strap off the steering oar with his teeth and swallowed it. He died a few hours later in convulsions. It was then decided by Chase, crewman Ben Lawrence and cabin boy Tom Nicholson, the only three left alive in Chase's boat, to eat Isaac Cole.

Captain Pollard's boat and Obed Hendrick's boat caught up with each other again after the storm. In Hendrick's boat, Charles Shorter died, and the crewmen decided unanimously to cut him up and eat him, which they did. A few nights later Pollard lost sight of Hendrick's boat. Hendrick and his crewmates were never seen again.

"What could we do?" asked Captain Pollard. *"We looked at each other with horrid thoughts in our minds."* When Lawson Thomas and Isaiah Shepard died in quick succession, they were devoured by the captain and his crewmates, the meat roasted over a fire kindled on the ballast sand in the bottom of the boat. With that food gone, on February 1 st the captain's horrid thoughts were put into action, and the living drew lots to see who would be sacrificed to feed the others — the cabin boy Owen Coffin lost the draw. He was killed by crewman Charles Ramsdell and eaten. A few days later, Samuel Reed died and Ramsdell and the captain proceeded to eat him too.

On February 16 the three in Owen Chase's boat were rescued by a passing ship, the British brig **INDIAN**. *"Two emaciated men and a feeble boy,"* reported the brig's commander William Crozier, *"came aboard looking little better than skeletons in trousers."* Seven days later, the two survivors in the captain's boat, Pollard and Ramsdell, sighted land, Santa Maria Island off the coast of Chile. They had been adrift for 95 days and had traveled 3,700 miles. Sailing in, they were spotted and picked up by, of all ships, the whaler **DAUPHIN** out of Nantucket, commanded by, of all people, Zimri Coffin, uncle of Owen Coffin, the cabin boy they had killed and just finished eating.

The three **ESSEX** crewmen who had remained on the island were rescued by the British ship **SURREY** in March of 1821. The **SURREY** was sent to the island by Captain Pollard, as he had promised. All eight survivors recovered to return to lives on the sea. The following year, however, Captain Pollard, commanding the whaler **TWO BROTHERS**, wrecked the ship on a reef in the South Pacific and ended up adrift in an open boat again. Although he was rescued a few days later, this second experience made him retire from whaling.

A sick joke made the rounds in Nantucket in the mid-1800's, when the horror of it all had somewhat subsided. The story, be it fact or fiction, is that a stranger came to Nantucket one day looking for his cousin Owen Coffin. He stopped to ask the town watchman, an elderly gentleman named George Pollard, if he knew Owen. *"Know him?"* shouted the watchman, *"Hell, man, I ate him !"*

Captain Pollard wasn't as shameless over the **ESSEX** *tragedy as* this story might indicate. He had fretful reoccurring nightmares for the rest of his life, as did many of the other survivors, and suffered with chronic indigestion — four of the eight survivors never ate meat again.

Boon Island, Maine, now with a lighthouse.

Old woodcut of a sperm whale attacking and sinking the ship **ESSEX** *of Nantucket in 1820.*

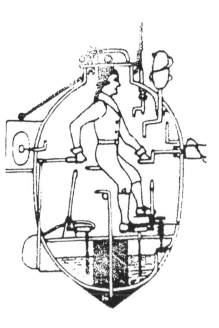

Sketch of Revolutionary War sub
TURTLE, by inventor David Bushnell.
John Holland's submarine FENIAN
RAM, and Simon Lake's clam digging
sub that rolled along the ocean bottom.

Face of clock, salvaged by divers from German U-Boat 853, off Rhode Island,
and Civil War sub HUNLEY. Photos by Paul Tzimoulis.

VI
STRANGE MACHINES CALLED SUBMARINES

The world's first submarine was built twenty years before Columbus discovered America. It was made of wood and had a small window through which its inventor, Robert Volturio of Venice, Italy, could view the underwater world. Volturio launched his box-like craft in the main street of his home town. The nortoriously murky waters of Venice prevented Volturio from seeing anything through his porthole. The submarine was submerged for only a short time before it started to leak; and soon, it fell apart.

The first successful submarine inventor was Cornelius Van Drebbel. He built a sub-surface rowboat, which he launched in the Thames River the same year the Pilgrims landed at Plymouth. The craft could swiftly cruise up and down the river at a depth of 15 feet with 12 husky men at the oars. It could remain underwater for three hours. People from miles around came to ride in Van Drebbel's rowboat — even England's King, James I, took an underwater cruise in it. Also, at first, hundreds of men volunteered to be oarsmen, but within a year, the novelty wore off. Oarsmen began complaining about rowing against swift currents, and many of them quit. Van Drebbel was forced to haul his submarine ashore; probably wondering why he had built the strange craft in the first place.

In 1774 another inventor tried to impress the King of England with a submersible boat. John Day informed the king and the local press that he would descend in his round wooden craft to a depth of 300 feet and remain there for an entire day. Many of the learned men of London informed Day that his submarine would be crushed by water pressures at that depth, but Day wouldn't listen. He entered his sub with a candle and a loaf of bread, waving at the crowd of hecklers that had gathered at dockside. He closed the hatch, lowered his craft into the sea, and neither he nor his submarine were ever seen again.

The inventor of America's first submarine was David Bushnell of Saybrook, Connecticut. When the American Revolution began, he was a student at Yale, where he had been experimenting extensively with gun powder. Bushnell decided to contribute to the fight for independence by building a machine that could transport explosives underwater. Within a few months he designed and constructed a strange looking egg-shaped submarine which he called the **TURTLE**. It had a vertical propeller that allowed the sub to rise and descend and a second prop which pushed the craft forward at a speed of 2 knots an hour. Only one man could fit inside the **TURTLE**, and he would have to breathe through two snorkel tubes that extended to the surface. When the **TURTLE** was submerged, the operator could peer into the sea through a small glass port hole. The man who volunteered to be America's first submariner was Ezra Lee, a sergeant in the Colonial Army.

A few weeks after the **TURTLE** was constructed, Bushnell received a letter from George Washington which read: *"Bring the water machine to New York to attack the British fleet..."* The Redcoats were overrunning Long Island and British Admiral Howe's man-o-wars threatened the coast.

The **TURTLE** arrived at Whitehall Stairs near the tip of Manhattan on September 6, 1776. Ezra Lee climbed aboard, and cruising along the surface, directed America's first sub toward the flotilla of British ships anchored off Staten Island. Two hours later, the partially submerged **TURTLE** bumped the hull of Admiral Howe's flagship, **H.M.S. EAGLE**. A sailor aboard the **EAGLE** spotted the submarine, but he didn't report it for he thought the **TURTLE** was nothing but an old wine barrel. Below, Ezra Lee was operating a mechanical drill in an attempt to puncture holes in the ship's bottom. Once the holes were drilled, he was to attach to the **EAGLE** a metal box of explosives on a time-charge — but the British had outsmarted the Colonials. The hull of the **EAGLE** was sheathed with copper and the **TURTLE**'s drill wouldn't bite into the metal. Lee was forced to retreat, but as he peddled the **TURTLE** back to shore, he was spotted by the Redcoats, who pursued in a row boat. As the British boat approached the submarine, Lee released his box of explosives, and although the explosives caused no casualties, it did send the Redcoats in fast retreat.

Yankee whaleboats intercepted the **TURTLE**, and America's first submariner was found unconscious inside. A few months later, Ezra Lee was at the controls of the **TURTLE** again, attacking British ships off the Virginia coast, but again, the mission failed. However, after the war, President George Washington said: *"I then thought and still think the TURTLE was an effort of genius."* Bushnell was disappointed that the **TURTLE** didn't succeed in destroying enemy ships, but his invention did make two important contributions to nautical science — it proved that gunpowder could be exploded underwater and that a screw propeller was an excellent method of propelling a craft in the water.

In a New Jersy river, one hundred years later, America launched another submarine. It slid down the ways, and as it hit the water, many spectators cheered; but the sub kept on going down and down and soon bubbled out of sight. Someone had forgotten to plug two vent holes in the sub's hull. She quickly filled with water and sank to the bottom. No one was injured in the accident, but the sub's designer and builder, an Irishman named John Holland, was very embarrassed. Holland salvaged his submarine and, three years later, launched it again in Brooklyn, New York. This time the inventor was aboard to see that nothing went wrong, but as the submarine began its dive, Holland heard the spectators shout a warning. He quickly brought the sub to the surface and opened the hatch to see what was wrong. There, clutching the submarine turret and holding on for dear life, was a frightened young black boy. Holland calmed the boy's fears and invited him into the sub. The hatch was closed and the sub submerged. An hour later, Holland surfaced his craft next to two men who were fishing in a rowboat. He wanted the men to row the boy back to shore. When the fishermen saw the submarine rise out of the sea and the man and boy climb out on deck, they rowed as swiftly as possible back toward shore. When they reached the dock, they ran to a nearby police station and reported seeing *". . . the devil and his disciple spit up from the mouth of a sea dragon . . ."*

The American government showed little interest in Holland's first submarines, and since his native land of Ireland was having *"troubles"* with the British, which always seems to be the case, he decided to build two undersea battle boats for Ireland. The biggest of the two subs was the **FENIAN RAM**, which measured 33 feet in length. The second was the **FENIAN RAM, JR.**, measuring only 16 feet in length. Both subs were completed in the winter of 1883. On a cold night, two of John Holland's cronies, slightly intoxicated, decided to steal the submarines and deliver them to Ireland. They boarded the **FENIAN RAM** and took **JUNIOR** in tow. Cruising along the surface, they made their way from New Jersy to Connecticut. In Long Island Sound they encountered rough weather and the **FENIAN RAM, JR.** swamped. The two Irishmen were forced to cut the tow line, and the miniature sub sank into the depths near Norwalk. Operating the second sub, the two thieves, trying to build up their courage to cross the Atlantic, cruised up and down Connecticut rivers. They were finally spotted and arrested by local police. The **FENIAN RAM** was confiscated as a menace to navigation, and the Irishmen were imprisoned. The submarine is now on display at Westside Park, Patterson, New Jersy. The **FENIAN RAM, JR.** remains underwater.

A few miles from where the **FENIAN RAM, JR.** sank, Simon Lake, another famous inventor, was designing and building submarines.

In 1895 he constructed a wooden submarine at Bridgeport, Connecticut that rolled along the ocean bottom on wheels. It also had an airlock through which passengers could pick oysters and clams off the sea bottom. In 1892, when the U.S. Navy asked inventors to submit plans for war-type submarines, Simon Lake and John Holland both complied. The Navy preferred Lake's design over Holland's, but later decided not to build a submarine after all. In 1895 the Navy requested sub designs once again, and, this time, Holland won out over Lake.

Holland built a submarine called the **PLUNGER** for the Navy. Although Holland protested, the government officials insisted that Navy engineers incorporate some of their ideas into his sub. The result was that the engines inside the **PLUNGER** generated so much heat that the crew couldn't stand being inside her for more than fifteen minutes while she was submerged. The Navy reneged on the contract, and the 85-foot **PLUNGER** was discarded. In 1900 the U.S. government became interested in submarines again, mainly because France, Spain, Germany, Italy and Greece had begun to build submarine fleets. America's submarine navy was born on April 11, 1900 when the government bought the submarine **HOLLAND** from John Holland for $150,000. Holland had previously built the submarine with private funds.

Both Holland and Lake built submarines for the British Navy, but before Simon Lake received an American contract, he was approached by the Russians and the Japanese. Russia and Japan were at war in 1904, and both nations wanted Lake submarines. Lake decided to sell to the Russians but knew that Japanese agents were watching his every move. One evening he managed to smuggle his submarine **PROTECTOR** out of Connecticut and into New York, where it was loaded onto a Russia bound ship. The submarine was registered as a cargo of coal. Simon Lake and his wife escorted the **PROTECTOR** to Russia, where they remained for seven years, continuously being wined and dined by the Czar. Although Lake's sub was never used against the Japanese, he received an order to build five more for the Russian Navy.

John Holland was also building submarines for the Rissians. One named the **FULTON** was smuggled to Russia, taken apart piece by piece at Kronstadt and transported in sections to Siberia, where it was reassembled again. A year later, Holland sold five subs to the Japanese. His assistant, Frank Cable, not only went to Tokyo to assemble the undersea boats, but he spent months teaching the Japanese Navy how to effectively use the subs in battle.

Five years later Frank Cable realized his mistake — America was now on the brink of war with Japan. Five American submarines were alerted and their skippers received orders which read: *"Proceed to Colon, Panama without stopping at any port en route, there remove the engines and batteries from the submarines, the hulls to be hauled up on the beach, the engines, batteries and hulls placed on flat cars, transported across the Isthmus by rail to Balboa, there to be reassembled for services in the Pacific in waters adjacent to the Panama Canal — for the purpose of repelling possible attacks by the Japanese Navy."* The American submarines departed on their mission from Cuba on Sunday, December 7, 1913. They were to defend the building of the Panama Canal, which the Japanese vehemently opposed, but the tense situation didn't explode in 1913. However — it did culminate **exactly** 28 years later — when the Japanese attacked Pearl Harbor with airplanes and submarines on Sunday, December 7, 1941.

John Holland of New Jersy and Simon Lake of Connecticut provided America, Russia, Japan and Britain with the world's first successful undersea boats. Because, some 33 years before Pearl Harbor, Frank Cable taught the Japanese how to construct and operate submarines, all the powerful nations of the world were prepared for undersea battle. The submarine was no longer a toy, but a destructive unseen weapon of war.

Submarine S-4, sank off Cape Cod in 1927.

VII
SAGA OF SUNKEN SUBS

The American submarine S-51 was rammed by the steamer CITY OF ROME off the Rhode Island coast on September 25, 1925. The helmsman aboard the steamer had spotted the sub's periscope skimming the water, but did not have time to alter course. The CITY OF ROME rode over the S-51, crushing her hull forward of the conning tower. Within 50 seconds the sub flooded and sank to a depth of 132 feet. The captain of the steamer radioed to shore the location of her sinking, which later proved to be incorrect, and he continued on his course to Boston. Three submariners who had been asleep in the battery room managed to escape through the conning tower hatch and were picked up on the surface by a passing ship one hour later. Seven others escaped from the sub but were found dead on the surface. The sunken S-51's location was found when oilslick was spotted on the choppy surface waters, and a diver was sent down to a depth of 132 feet with hoses to pump air into the trapped men. After tapping out signals on the hull without response from inside, the diver concluded that the remaining submariners were dead. Nine months later, the S-51 was raised and brought back to dry dock. All together, 33 men of the S-51 lost their lives. Ironically, the number 33 becomes mysteriously prominent in all future New England submarine disasters.

Two years later, December 17, 1927, the submarine S-4 collided with the U.S. Coast Guard destroyer PAULDING. As the PAULDING scoured the waters off Provincetown, Massachusetts looking for rum runners, she smashed into something which her deck officer first thought was a fisherman's marker. Actually it was the conning tower of the S-4. The sub sank in 110 feet of water with 40 men trapped inside her. The PAULDING's skipper immediately reported the accident, and salvage boats with divers aboard were rushed to the scene.

Diver Tom Eadie volunteered to dive first. Wearing hard-hat diving equipment with an air-hose connected to a surface compressor, he descended through 100 feet of murky water and landed in the center of the S-4's superstructure. Diver Eadie then listened as the submariners tapped out a message to him on the inner hull — *"seven men alive in torpedo compartment,"* they reported in Morse Code — *"33 dead in other flooded compartments. Is there any hope?"*

"Yes," Eadie hammered in return. *"Your families are praying for you — don't give up hope."*

For two days divers attempted to raise the S-4 by pumping compressed air into into her ballast tanks. The salvage ships pitched in wild seas as the divers worked against time in the turbulent waters below. As one salvage diver attempted to connect an air hose to the sub, he lost his balance, fell and was pinned to the wreckage. On the surface, Tom Eadie was called out of the salvage ship's decompression chamber to help his fellow diver. Eadie descended and found his partner unconcious, with water flooding his diving suit. It took Eadie two hours to free the other diver and drag him to the surface. Both men were in such critical condition that the surface boat had to leave the scene and rush them to the hospital. Below, the seven submariners tapped out their last message — *"All is well."* Three months later, when the S-4 was salvaged, their bodies were found in the air-tight torpedo compartment. Because of his valiant efforts in trying to save the men of the S-4, and for saving the life of his diving partner, Tom Eadie was awarded the Congressional Medal of Honor, America's highest award for bravery.

After the S-4 disaster, the British and Americans were prompted to conceive easier escapes for submariners. The British installed rapid flood valves in their submarines for quicker escapes and to help avoid the dreaded *"bends,"* caused by breathing nitrogen under pressure for an extended period of time. The Americans invented and built a rescue diving chamber called the McCann Bell. It was shaped like a pear, could be lowered into the water on a cable from a surface ship, and connected to the hatch of a disabled submarine. Trapped men could open the submarine hatch, climb into the bell without getting wet, and be raised to the surface. The McCann Bell was used successfully eleven years after the S-4 went down.

The American patrol submarine **SQUALUS** sank on May 12, 1939, only eleven days after her launching. She was making her first dive off the coast of Portsmouth, New Hampshire when water began flooding her stern compartments. The sub commander immediately tried to surface the 300-foot craft, but she sank deeper and deeper, until she struck bottom at a depth of 240 feet. The flooding stern compartments were bolted shut by order of the commander, trapping and drowning 26 of the 59 men aboard. The 33 men in the air-tight bow section released a smoke bomb and a yellow buoy to the surface. Written on the buoy, which was attached by line to the sub was, *"Sub SQUALUS sank here. Telephone Inside."* The submarine **SCULPIN**, sister ship of the **SQUALUS**, found the buoy bobbing on the surface and her commander reported the location to the Naval Base at Portsmouth. A convoy of ships converged on the spot and rescue operations began.

On the morning of May 13 a navy hard-hat diver was sitting on the deck of the SQUALUS directing the ten-ton McCann Bell to the forward hatch cover. Once connected to the sub, the trapped submariners were able to open the hatch and climb into the bell - 33 members of the SQUALUS crew were thus saved. The submarine was salvaged and exactly one year later was again launched from the Portsmouth Navy Yard. Her new name was SAILFISH, but her crew knew she was the old SQUALUS, and they nicknamed her "SQUALFISH."

During World War II, the SAILFISH sank seven enemy ships, including the Japanese carrier CHUYO. Unknown to the SAILFISH crew at the time, 21 American submariners from the SCULPIN were aboard the CHUYO as prisoners of war. When the torpedo from the old SQUALUS sank the CHUYO, the SCULPIN crew went down with her. These were the same men who had found the sunken SQUALUS off Portsmouth three years earlier and had helped rescue 33 members of her crew.

A second submarine disaster occured off Portsmouth, New Hampshire on June 16, 1941 at a spot only a few miles from where the SQUALUS sank. The training sub 0-9 crashed out of control into crushing depths some 14 miles off the Isles of Shoals. No one knows what caused the 0-9 to sink, but all hope of rescue was soon abandoned. A naval funeral was held at the site for the 33 men who were aboard her when she sank.

Let us leave New England for one story about a British submarine, because she shared an eerie coincidence with the SQUALUS and is one of several submarines outside of New England waters where the number 33, or its multiple, was mysteriously prominent during an underwater disaster.

Britain's new submarine THETIS was on her maiden voyage off the coast of England in June of 1939 — only three weeks after the SQUALUS tragedy off Portsmouth. Aboard were 53 officers and crewmen, plus 50 engineers and workmen who were along to check the performance of this new addition to the British Navy. Some 14 miles at sea, Commander Oram gave the order to dive. Unknowingly, one of the torpedo tube doors was left open and water came pouring into the sub at a rate of two tons per second. The THETIS quickly sank to the bottom, bow first, and settled into the mud at a depth of 160 feet. With most bow compartments flooded, Commander Oram ordered the stern to be lightened of all materials. The commander wisely reckoned that the moving of heavy items from the stern to the unflooded bow compartments would keep the near panicked civilians occupied, and would allow the stern of the 275 foot sub to rise above the surface waters.

It was only a few hours later that the **THETIS** was at an 80 degree angle, with part of her stern exposed above the water. The skipper of a fishing trawler spotted it and radioed to shore for help. When Commander Oram heard sound of props overhead, he allowed two submariners to make a free ascent through the escape hatch. They made it to the surface and were rescued. A few minutes later, three more men flooded the escape hatch to get away; but the hatch door jammed, and they were drowned. Two others managed to open the door again — they made it to the surface. The many trapped men breathing the limited air inside the **THETIS**, however, soon caused the air to turn foul. Before anyone else could attempt an escape, they were asphixiated. Only four **THETIS** men lived — one was Commander Oram. The remaining 99 perished inside the sunken sub.

Five months later the **THETIS** was salvaged and towed ashore. She was cleaned out, repainted, and, like the **SQUALUS**, renamed. It was war time, and the British could not afford to dispose of a fit submarine. The **THUNDERBOLT**, ex-**THETIS**, was ready for action, but the chore was to find a new commander and crew willing to serve on a seemingly *"jinxed"* submarine. The new commander, C.B. Crouch, and his crew were volunteers. All declared to the Admiralty that they were not superstitious — most of these volunteers were tough ex-convicts.

The **THUNDERBOLT** went to war, and by December 1, 1940 had destroyed two German U-Boats. While on patrol, she also managed to pick up 43 British sailors who Commander Crouch had spotted through his periscope floundering on the surface. The sailors were survivors of a merchant ship destroyed by a U-boat torpedo. Once aboard the submarine, one rescued sailor went beserk. *"My brother died in this submarine,"* he screamed, *"and I feel him still here."*

When the **THUNDERBOLT** arrived at Gibraltar to deliver her 43 passengers, four of the submarine's crewmen requested a transfer — they had concluded the **THUNDERBOLT** was haunted. Commander Crouch granted their transfer. On the day before the **THUNDERBOLT** was to leave Gibraltar on her next war patrol, another crewman requested a transfer. He told the commander of a letter he had received from his wife, reading in part: *"I had a strange dream and saw you dead..."* Commander Crouch told this seaman that it was too late for him to leave; he had no replacement for him. Crouch now had 65 men and could not run the submarine efficiently with less.

The night before the THUNDERBOLT departed, Crouch was awakened by two British Naval officers who rudely entered his cabin. *"You must not sail in the THETIS,"* said one. *"This is the THUNDER-BOLT,"* replied Crouch. *"It is the THETIS,"* said the other, and they both then left the commander's cabin. Commander Crouch reported the incident to his land-based superiors at Gibraltar next morning. The identity of these two officers was never determined and Crouch reluctantly agreed the experience must have been a bad dream. Only moments before the THUNDERBOLT left Gibraltar, however, Crouch received a letter from his wife which read in part: *". . . I have a feeling the THUNDERBOLT won't come back from this trip . . ."* With all these forwarnings, the THUNDERBOLT cruised out into the Mediterranean on March 12. One day later, March 13, 1943 while in the process of torpedoing a German merchant ship, the submarine was spotted by enemy planes. She was bombed, quickly sank to the bottom, and with her went 66 submariners, including Commander Crouch. There were no survivors.

On the evening if May 2, 1945, German Admiral Doenitz sent a message out to all Nazi ships ordering them to cease hostilities and return to home bases. Perhaps Helmut Froemdorf, Commander of the U-boat U-853 of the 33rd subflotila, never heard the order as he cruised his submarine off the coast of Rhode Island. Three days later he sent two torpedos into the American collier BLACK POINT in Naragan-sett Bay. The collier sank, taking down 12 crewmen with her. Later that day, crewmen aboard a Yugoslavian ship sighted the U-853 on the surface near Block Island, seemingly launching men in rubber liferafts. The American destroyer ERICKSON was quickly on the scene; spotted the U-853 making a dive, and blasted her with depth charges. Geysers of oil and bits of debris came to the surface, along with Commander Froemdorf's cap and chart table. Froemdorf, eight officers and 33 German crewmen lost their lives. It was May 6, only nine hours before Germany officially surrendered to the allies.

Eighteen years later, the worst submarine disaster in history occurred 220 miles off the coast of Boston, Massachusetts. The world's fastest and deepest diving nuclear submarine, U.S.S. THRESHER, sank like a boulder to a crusing depth of 8,400 feet. She was on her third day of diving tests off the coast — it was 9:00 AM, April 10, 1963, and the crew of the subtender SKYLARK watched the 278-foot

THRESHER dive below the choppy surface waters. She was to submerge to a depth of approximately 1,200 feet — her maximum depth capacity was about 2,000 feet. At 9:13 AM, the **SKYLARK** received a message from the **THRESHER**'s radioman: *"Approaching test depth — experiencing minor difficulty — have up angle — attempting to blow up . . ."* Then the message was garbled and the **SKYLARK** receiver emitted a strange crackling sound — the sounds of the **THRESHER** being crushed on her final, fatal dive.

Aboard her were 129 men: 113 naval officers and enlisted men, 13 civilian technicians from the Portsmouth Naval Shipyard, and three private contractors. There should have been 133 men aboard her that morning, but fate saved four of the **THRESHER** crew — Crewman Frank DeStefano and Raymond Mattson were on sick leave; Crewman Stanley Weitzel was on temporary transfer to navigational school; and Lieutenant Raymond McCoole had been called home at the last minute, his wife accidentally spilled rubbing alcohol in her eyes, causing temporary blindness. McCoole had to care for his children while his wife recuperated. It would have been his first dive on the **THRESHER** — and his last.

United States President John F. Kennedy said, *"The **THRESHER** pioneered a new era in the eternal drama of the sea, diving deeper and going faster than any submarine before it."* She was also built to attack surface ships and enemy shore bases with homing torpedoes and missiles, without having to raise her periscope; but with all her capabilities, she experienced difficulties from the start. Only one year after her launching on July 9, 1960, she caught fire while on a shakedown cruise off Charleston, South Carolina. The fire, caused by an overheated motor, was extinguished, but there were a few fearful minutes for commander and crew. A year later, June 5, 1962, the **THRESHER** was rammed by the tug **HOLLYWOOD** at Port Canveral, Florida. With a three-foot gash in her ballast tank, she returned to Groton, Connecticut for repairs. In October of that year, she was sent to Portsmouth for six more months of major overhauling, for the **THRESHER** suffered a series of malfunctions during test dives. The fatal dive in April 1963 was her first deep water dive after being overhauled. Ironically, the morning she sank, Navy sub bases throughout the country were holding memorial services for the 1,500 submariners who lost their lives during World War II.

Only 13 months after the **THRESHER** disaster, May 13, 1964, three nuclear submarines were being celebrated at the Portsmouth, New Hampshire Naval Shipyard: commissioning of the **JOHN ADAMS**, with 1,300 people gathered for the ceremony; keel-laying ceremonies for the submarine **GRAYLING**; and the launching of the **NATHAN-AEL GREENE**. Thousands were gathered for the latter two events as well. This was the first triple ceremony ever conducted at the Portsmouth shipyard. Suddenly cries of horror were heard. A high-voltage wire had whipped down from a staging, striking six workmen standing under the bow of the **NATHANEL GREENE**. All were knocked to the ground; one of them, a rigger named Sam Falcone, was electrocuted instantly. Ambulances rushed to the scene and delivered the other five badly burned men to the hospital. The ceremony was halted. The **NATHANEL GREENE** was the 133rd submarine built and launched at the Portsmouth shipyard.

It was only 20 days after the **THRESHER** was launched on June 9, 1960 that the 253-foot nuclear powered attack submarine **SCORPION** was commissioned into the U.S. Navy. She was designed to search out and fight enemy submarines underwater and was named after a World War II sub that was lost in the Pacific in 1944. It was not long before the **SCORPION** established an underwater endurance record by remaining submerged for 70 consecutive days without surfacing. In January 1967, she struck fear into the British Admiralty when on joint maneuvers off England she failed to respond to a radio message ordering her to surface. It was 48 hours later that the **SCORPION** responded and broke radio silence to inform the British Navy that she had not met the same fate as the **THRESHER**. The **SCORPION** commander had simply misinterpreted the rules of the war games.

A year later, while on maneuvers in the Mediterranean, the **SCORPION** commander, 36 year old Francis Slattery, offered to assist in the search for two submarines — one French and one Israeli — that had mysteriously disappeared. The 1,040-ton French sub **MINERVE** with 54 men aboard sank off Toulon on January 28 for unknown reasons. The previous day, off Cyprus — the opposite end of the Mediterranean — the 1,280-ton Israeli sub **DAKAR (SHARK)** disappeared. She had been traveling from Portsmouth, England from Haifa with 128 people aboard. Neither sub was found.

Four months later, while returning to Norfolk, Virginia from her unsuccesful search mission in the Mediterranean, the **SCORPION** vanished. Her last message to the Navy was on May 21, 1968 as she cruised off the Azores. She then maintained radio silence. It was normal for submarines making a submerged passage to remian silent for extended periods of time, but on May 27, when the **SCORPION** had still not arrived at Norfolk, the Navy announced that she was missing. Ships, submarines and planes made an extensive five-month search of the Atlantic; but it was not until October 31, 1968 that the **SCORPION** was located by the research ship **MIZAR**. **SCORPION** was 10,000 feet down, 400 miles southwest of the Azores. Cameras and strobe lights were dropped into these two-mile depths and resulting photos showed that her hull and bow sections were intact, but photos did not reveal any clues as to why the submarine sank.

There were 99 men aboard the **SCORPION** when she met her end. Like the ill-fated submarines before her, the number 33 was again mysteriously present. Let us hope she was the last in this strange undersea saga of sunken submarines.

Submarine and sub-tender search the waters off Boston for wreckage from the ill-fated nuclear submarine THRESHER. She sank to a depth of one and one-half miles, in 1963.
Photo courtesy the Boston Globe.